The Land and People of
BELGIUM

Since ancient Roman times, Belgium has often been used as a battle-ground by foreign armies. But the location and topography that made this small nation so accessible to invaders has also made it an important center for trade and industry, and its capital, Brussels, is today the home of many international organizations.

Although very much a part ot today's world, Belgium preserves its past. Treasures of painting and architecture recall a rich heritage of art and craftsmanship, and the presence of two distinct cultures—Flemish (Dutch-speaking) and Walloon (French-speaking)—reflects Belgium's eventful political history. In this new revision, the author traces the events and forces that shaped the country and describes the Belgium of today.

PORTRAITS OF THE NATIONS SERIES

Also in the same format

The Land and People of
BELGIUM

by Dorothy Loder

REVISED EDITION 1973

PORTRAITS OF THE NATIONS SERIES

J. B. LIPPINCOTT COMPANY
Philadelphia   New York

13435680

For permission to reproduce the photographs on the following pages, the author gratefully credits: Institut Belge d'Information et de Documentation, Brussels, pages 13, 22, 30, 37, 40, 71, 103, 117. Official Belgian Tourist Bureau, New York, pages 15, 19, 48, 52, 54, 67, 68, 77, 79, 81, 86, 87, 91, 97, 99, 106, 109, 112, 122, 124, 133.

U.S. Library of Congress Cataloging in Publication Data

Loder, Dorothy.
  The land and people of Belgium.

  (Portraits of the nations series)
  SUMMARY: An introduction to the history and people of Belgium, the tiny country frequently called the Crossroads of Europe.
  1. Belgium—Juvenile literature. [1. Belgium] I. Title.
DH434.L63   1973   914.93'03'4   72-13301
ISBN-0-397-31462-0

Contents

Author's Note

Belgium is a bilingual country; the Walloons speak French, and the Flemish speak Flemish (Dutch, Netherlandish). Belgian geographical names exist in both languages, and occasionally in English as well. In the text of this book, geographical and place names conform with usage in the respective areas. In a few cases the more commonly known English equivalent (Antwerp, River Scheldt, Ostend, Brussels, Ghent) is used.

Foreword

Rarely have I read a more vivid, a more sparkling presentation of my country than in Mrs. Loder's *The Land and People of Belgium.* Indeed, her book blends up-to-date factual information together with an excellent historical evocation into a work which captivates the reader.

I am grateful to Mrs. Loder for this result, and I hope that the created interest may bring many readers to my country. Belgium being a land of transition between the Germanic and the Latin cultures, a country impregnated with a tradition of give-and-take, it is quite natural that the Belgians have been—and are—Europe's compromise initiators inside and outside the Common Market. The Belgians want to play the same role in the Atlantic Community, now more and more a reality.

Young America, this book brings you a message of friendship. Read it, come and see us, and help us bridge the Atlantic!

Herman J. Matsaert
Consul General of Belgium

Houston, Texas, 1973

1

The Crossroads

Belgians are noted for their sense of humor. During World
Wars I and II, they made dangerous fun of their German con-
querors and their misfortunes. Nowadays they quip about their
chilly, changeable weather; they ridicule politicians, judges, and
businessmen; they joke about the dangerous rift between Dutch-
speaking Flemings and French-speaking Walloons, even though
the gap between these main national groups widens from year to
year and has already changed the form of government to some extent.

But no Belgian is amused if you speak of "little Belgium." The
area of the country is indeed small. Reaching west from Germany
and southwest from the Grand Duchy of Luxembourg to the
North Sea and north from France to Holland, Belgium is not so
large as Holland and only slightly bigger than our state of Mary-
land. After Holland, however, it is the most densely populated
area in Europe, with over 9.5 million inhabitants, more than a
million of whom live in the capital city, Brussels. Physically, Belgium is a land of varied topography, graduating from North Sea
dikes and dunes to the plains of Flanders and rising ever higher
to gorges and forested hills in the Ardennes of Wallonia to the
southeast.

Whatever the element is that makes a country a melting pot, this ingredient is lacking in Belgium. The Flemish who people the seacoast and northern flatlands do not want to be like the Walloons, who flaunt their cultural differences and interests. To the east, the district incorporating the towns of Eupen and Malmédy was awarded Belgium at the close of World War I, then taken back by the Germans in World War II and returned again to Belgium only in 1945. Here, German-speaking people, a minority of less than one percent of the national population, treasures its own inheritance, listens to radio broadcasts in German, reads German-language papers and books, and sends its children to schools where classes are taught in German.

Despite this divided loyalty, Belgians take pride in their country's contribution to European civilization. A dozen cities contain splendid and historic buildings and such a wealth of painting, carving, and sculpture as to deserve the international reputation of art cities. Belgian crusaders, painters, musicians, writers, and patriots have enriched Western life.

For nearly a thousand years, the land played a great and often tragic part in European history. It has been the battleground for warring nations, which chose to meet on its soil rather than their own. Invaders and allies alike sowed Belgium with their dead. Near the old city of Tongeren (Tongres in French), thousands of Roman soldiers lie where they fell fighting those *Belgae* whom Julius Caesar described as "the fiercest of the tribes of Gaul." British and Prussian armies defeated Napoleon Bonaparte at Waterloo. The two World Wars of our century scattered cemeteries: British in Flanders, French along the River Meuse in the Ardennes region of Wallonia. Thousands of Americans lie buried not far from the town of Bastogne where they held off the Nazis in the Battle of the Bulge at Christmastime, 1944.

Since the Middle Ages, Belgians have been robbed and op-

A statue of the Virgin ornaments a building in Bruges.

pressed by enemies; they have seen fields ruined, cities looted and burned. Yet when smoke lifted and fighting ended, they replanted, rebuilt, and went back to normal, industrious lives. The farmer on his below-sea-level land, artisans beating out copperware in towns along the River Meuse, the diamond-cutter of Antwerp, the weaver of Ghent or Kortrijk (Courtrai), the small-town mayor—all of whom take their duties seriously—are typical of a people who cling to self-respect and tradition.

After the turmoil, it seems incredible that so much of the past and such a keen sense of national identity survive. Many buildings have been restored so carefully that here and there another age possesses a town. Bruges looks much as it did in the sixteenth century. One often has the illusion of long ago as one stands in a Grand'Place or Grote Markt (respectively French and Flemish for Main Square), flanked by a cathedral, bell tower, town hall, and the carved, perhaps gilded, houses of the guilds (tradesmen's unions). The past is mirrored in the water of a canal flowing between gabled bouses. It lurks behind the ramparts of a crusader's castle. It echoes in the music of ancient belfries.

Enemies found Belgium easy to invade because it had no natural frontiers for defense. Peacetime visitors realize how easily one travels there, veined as the land is with traffic-bearing rivers and canals, good roads, railways, and interurban trolleys. Barges ply the waters through Belgium and enter the North Sea from Holland. The Scheldt serves the ports of Antwerp and Ghent; the latter city enlarged and modernized its port in 1969. The city of Liège in the southeast is a shipping center, thanks to the Meuse and the Albert Canal. In the morning Liège can load a barge on the Meuse with steel or perhaps shipments of glass made in nearby Val Saint Lambert. That night, the steel and crystal will be in Antwerp, ready for transfer to ships bound for foreign ports. From Liège, having shunted its traffic into the Albert Canal, the Meuse sweeps north between white cliffs, old towns, and castles. Outlining the Belgian-Dutch border, it enters the sea at the Dutch port of Rotterdam.

The first European passenger trains ran in Belgium, shuttling between Brussels and nearby Mechelen (Malines). This was in 1835. Today the Belgian national railroad system is the densest in the world, covering the nation like a grid. Through Brussels pass trains en route to Germany, France, Holland, and beyond. Train-ferry service leaves direct from Brussels for London. Air and steamship lines bring in travelers and freight from the Americas, Africa, and other continents, while commercial helicopters link Brussels to cities in Belgium, France, and Germany.

The Belgian coast along the North Sea is a short trip from Brussels by train or highway. This region of stormy winters can be delightful when summer winds blow over the high dunes and tangle long strands of *oyat* grass planted to hold down the sand. The forty-odd miles of North Sea shore are strung with towns where, in summer, flags of the nine Belgian provinces fly over beaches crowded with visitors from every province, as well as with foreign vacationers. In Ostend (Oostende in Flemish), an internationally known seaside resort, crowds flock to the casino, the theater, the race track, the beaches. Meanwhile, the harbor carries on with its everyday work. Fishermen mend their nets on the shore

Women mending fishing nets in Oostende.

or unload slippery cargoes at the dock, as buyers jam the market where the catch is auctioned off. Boats prepare to put out to sea again. Ostend sole, caught in nearby waters, is a fish so delicate that restaurants as far away as the United States fly it over to serve as a special attraction. Some vessels put out for waters off Scotland and Denmark; others, the big trawlers, sail as far away as Iceland, four days' voyage into the foggy North Atlantic, to spend ten days there catching haddock and cod.

The polders lie behind dikes and dunes which stretch along both banks of the Scheldt after it leaves Antwerp, as well as the seacoast to the southwest. The towns of Veurne (Furnes), Ostend, and Knokke serve as marketing centers for produce raised on the farms which now cover this maritime plan. The polders, below sea level, have been built up by deposits of silt, sand, and rubble left by water. Drainage ditches crisscross this land. Roads run on causeways over meadows of lush grass, fat cattle graze here, and vegetables grow in narrow fields. Poplar trees lining the roads lean to the east, bent by strong sea winds from the west. Here and there a stand of evergreens or a cluster of apple and pear trees shades a brick farmhouse. An occasional windmill rises from the flat green expanse.

Inland, the polder belt changes to higher ground. Towns and villages scatter so thickly over the Flanders plain that one seems to crowd the next and you hear the bells of more than one community at the same time. Around Ghent (Gent in Flemish, Gand in French), "the city of flowers," stretch acres of greenhouses growing roses and orchids. Tulips and azaleas bloom outdoors in April and May; rhododendron follows, while begonias and roses of the fields make summer color. Around Kortrijk (Courtrai), southwest of Ghent, flax plants flower into blue lakes in June and July.

From the city of Antwerp (Antwerpen, Anvers), a district

known as the Kempen (Campine) stretches east through the province of Limburg to the Dutch border. Empty moors reach out for mile after mile, patched in yellow broom and purple heather, stitched with fir trees, and knotted with clumps of white birches. Some cattle graze here, but farms are not prosperous, for the land is poor and the Kempen was neglected for a long time. Now the picture is changing: coal mines discovered some years ago in parts of Limburg contain richer veins than the old, old mines of Wallonia in the south—some of the latter had been worked from the seventeenth century until recently. Belgian coal production has been sharply cut; less goes on even in the Kempen. Nevertheless, scars of mining remain. Other industries have since come along with foundries and smelters; now a big new steel mill clouds Kempen air with smoke and fumes.

Despite industry, much of the peaceful scene remains unspoiled. Southern Limburg is planted in orchards which April and May turn into bouquets of apple, pear, and plum blossoms. The ripe cherry crop draws buyers from as far away as England to the Limburg town of Sint Truiden (Saint Trond), where a cherry festival celebrates the harvest and cherry tarts are served everywhere.

Southeast of Brussels, in the province of Brabant, grape growers claim to have perfect bunches ripe every day of the year, for sweet black grapes form on vines protected by the glass of thousands of hothouses on southern slopes. Red-roofed villages stand among fields of wheat, barley, hops, and sugar beets. Here and there, a farmer drives a tractor through his fields, but one also sees him working Brabantine horses; Belgium still has some eighty thousand horses. These beautiful animals have smoothly rounded body and butterscotch-colored coat trimmed in long, creamy tail and mane.

Waterloo, the scene of Napoleon Bonaparte's final defeat, is situated on the imaginary line which cuts Belgium into two almost equal sections. To the north and west lies the Flanders sector, while the Wallonia region extends south and east. The provinces of East and West Flanders, plus Limburg, Antwerp, and North Brabant, constitute the land of Flanders; Wallonia comprises Southern Brabant, Hainaut, Namur, Liège and Luxembourg, not to be confused with the independent Grand Duchy of the same name. In 1962, a law passed by parliament fixed this linguistic frontier. More than a geographic marker, it has become a battle line between warring ideas and ambitions of Flemish and Walloons.

For generations, heavy industry concentrated south of the frontiers, and parts of Wallonia remain industrialized. Although less than half the amount of coal mined in the 1950's is brought out today, cities like Mons and Charleroi, as well as Liège, still show the grime of mines, the dust of quarries; smoke from furnaces clouds the air, hillocks of slag blotch the landscape.

Wallonia is not all factory towns. Much of it unrolls miles of scenery that grows wider as it slants southeast to the Ardennes, a land of wooded hills, narrow valleys, and green vistas extending through the southern and eastern provinces. In streams of the Ardennes, fishermen catch trout and grayling, which tastes like trout. In the forests, hunters bag quail, pheasants, and grouse in season, or they stalk deer and wild sheep. All year through, one may kill a wild boar. Now and again someone shoots a wolf.

The Ardennes is a summer playground for many who camp, fish, and drink the waters of mineral springs. Valleys shelter communities of white, green, and blue camper vans. The name of the town of Spa has become a word in the dictionary, a resort where one goes to drink the waters. For centuries, Spa entertained kings and queens, the rich and fashionable from all over Europe, but now it attracts few notables, and most of the expensive hotels have been replaced by inns for working people. If, traveling through Belgium, one calls for bottled water, as so many Europeans do, one can order nothing more delicious than a bottle of Spa, carbonated or uncarbonated.

The rivers flow to musical names like the Lesse, the Ourthe,

The casino at Spa, a luxurious watering place.

the Semois, the Ninglinspo. On their way to join the Meuse they tumble down ravines or leap in cascades, sometimes meandering when they reach a valley city like Bouillon. The Lesse has carved out the Caverns of Han into a magic palace glimmering in underground darkness. A three-hour boat trip passes through the caverns—whose chambers have such names as the Alhambra, Boudoir of Persephone, Hall of the Dome—where stalactites drip from the roof and stalagmites heap up fantastic landscapes. This is an entirely different world from that of a canal trip from Bruges to a village like Damme.

Belgium deserves more attention from the average American tourist than it receives. Often a visitor omits it from his tour of Europe or, at most, spends a day or two in Brussels, makes a hurried visit to Bruges and Ghent, and then is off to Paris or Vienna or Rome. On the other hand, travelers interested in art or those who want to hear good music know Belgium well. Businessmen examine it as a field for investment; more than eleven hundred large American companies operate there. Military men and diplomats know it as the nerve center of present-day European planning.

2

The Family Name Is Belgium

Looking at the Belgian coat of arms, one sees a motto below the lion to the left of the shield and another under the lion at the right. The words on the left, *L'Union Fait la Force,* are French, whereas on the right *Eendracht Maakt Macht* says the same thing in Flemish. Both mean "In Union There Is Strength." Ironically, this double motto seems rather to show the divided feeling of French- and Flemish-speaking groups in the nation. Flemings, whose numbers have grown faster than the Walloons, amount to 60 percent of Belgium's population, or about 4.5 million people, while slightly more than 3 million Walloons constitute the other 40 percent. The German community in Liège Province numbers only about sixty thousand persons.

Theoretically, Flemings and Walloons contrast in appearance, temperament, and talents, as well as in language, although, in fact, many Belgians are of mixed inheritance. Thirty out of every hundred marriages performed today are between Flemings and Walloons. A typical Fleming is sturdy, blue-eyed with golden or reddish hair, possibly handsome. Walloons, too, when true to type, have their special good looks. They are darker, with clear skin and smaller frames; sometimes they resemble the Welsh. This is understandable, because like the Welsh they descend in part from Celtic tribes that spread in prehistoric times over Europe and intermarried with Germanic settlers. The Flemish word *Waals*, meaning "Walloon," comes from the same root as *Welsh*. Walloons may even have a dash of Roman blood, because Rome gov-

A flower farm in East Flanders.

erned their region of Belgium. The typical Fleming is apt to be pious, conservative, stubborn, hardworking, yet friendly and plea-sure-loving; when angry, he is hostile. Words like *lively, gay, restless—friendly*, too—describe a typical Walloon, who, like a Fleming, is ready to fight at the least excuse.

In the past, Flemings worked alone or in small groups at pains-taking crafts handed down from one generation to the next. To some extent, they still create beautiful piecework. They are not merely industrious; they are talented as well. Practically all the celebrated Belgian painters came from Flanders. The textile in-dustry, in the modern sense of the word, is the oldest in Europe —and what beautiful textiles! The art of lace-making began in Flanders; women make lace by hand, though not much any more, because the work is tedious and therefore lace costs too much for many purchasers. Men fashion musical instruments and turn out furniture, though furniture, too, is often machine-made today.

Originally, heavy industry predominated in Wallonia, due per-haps to the discovery of coal and iron there long before similar discoveries in Flanders. In the past, Walloons received better sci-entific and engineering training than Flemings, because of rolling mills, gun and locomotive works, quarries, and coal mines in their region. By now, however, industry in the north has largely overtaken existing business in the south, for the pattern has changed. Coal mines in the Kempen and the fine seaports of Ant-werp and Ghent, as well as Zeebrugge on the North Sea, attract vast investments. Antwerp and Ghent have refineries and fertil-izer and chemical plants, also machine works, which are more modern and efficient than those older establishments to the south.

When Belgium became an independent nation in 1830, French became the official language for a number of reasons. Upper-class Flemings had long used French as naturally as the Walloons, for the land of Flanders had in theory been part of France through a long period of time, certainly until the sixteenth century. Some counts of Flanders are said to have been unable to talk with those of their humble subjects who knew only Flemish. Even after the country became the Spanish Netherlands, French dominated polite society and diplomacy. Merchants, nobles, churchmen in the north associated with Frenchmen from their class as well as with natives of other lands, who also spoke French.

If you think it unfair to have ignored the speech of rural districts and narrow back streets, remember that Flemish, though now again like Dutch as it is correctly spoken, broke into a jumble of dialects among the uneducated, hard to understand from one province to the next. This situation no longer exists; in Flanders all social classes now speak Dutch again.

In addition to standard French, Wallonia also cherishes dialects which resemble Old French of a thousand years ago and contain many Germanic words. Learned societies study the different versions of this speech; amateur players stage Walloon plays. Students at the University of Liège are said to know countless regional songs, which they sing when they gather in club or cafe. One might say that, like the Flemings, Walloons have the old speech in their blood. A young man in Brussels, whose family came to the capital from the Ardennes several generations ago, once remarked, "We never speak anything but French at home unless my mother is angry. Then she scolds us in Walloon dialect."

Education has standardized Netherlandish and for years the language has been legally recognized. A few decades back, government, the courts, and the army functioned only in French. Judges often did not understand the speech of an accused in a courtroom in Flanders. During World War I boys from Flanders served under officers who could not communicate with them; they could not understand the commands they heard nor read directions printed in a strange language; they grew confused and resentful. All government posts must now be filled by applicants who are bilingual.

Some ardent Flamingants (men who agitated for recognition of Flemish language and culture) were partly French. Hendrik Conscience, ignoring the fact that his sailor father was a Frenchman and prizing only his inheritance from a Flemish mother, wrote a novel in Dutch, *The Lion of Flanders,* which praised the bravery of Flanders in its early fourteenth-century struggle against France. The book thrilled the Flamingants and, although first published nearly a hundred years ago, is still read. Its title refers to the black lion rearing on the coat of arms of the counts of Flanders. A stirring song, also titled "The Lion of Flanders," has become a hymn, dearer perhaps to the Flemish than the Belgian national anthem, "La Brabançonne" (The Song of Brabant). This may be due in part to the fact that "La Brabançonne" has entirely different French and Flemish lyrics. Its music, incidentally, was written by a composer with a Flemish name. He may or may not have been a Fleming, but he certainly used French because he named the song in that language.

Although a few miles north of the linguistic frontier, Brussels exists as a separate entity in the language-cultural disputes. Statistics often run as follows: Flemings 4.5 million, a few more than 3 million Walloons, Brussels between 1 million and 1.5 million. You hear more French than Flemish spoken; some authorities claim four-fifths of the Bruxellois use French as their first language. Nevertheless one does hear a good deal of Flemish today in offices and stores. All street signs and other notices appear in both languages. Though most government officials speak French, the pattern is changing, if only because of rules for bilingual government service. Whereas a Fleming invariably chooses French as a second language in school, Walloons often prefer to study English or German, both of which they consider more important from an economic and social viewpoint.

The Flemish resent this indifference. Partisans in the dispute disagree with each other in every field, and though the quarrel has been blown up by politicians and may not reflect the feelings of many Belgians, who genuinely like each other, it has already changed the very form of government. Now the cabinet contains a minister for French culture and another minister for Flemish culture. To the anger of many Bruxellois, parliament, although still recognizing the bilingual status of the city's nineteen *communes* or districts, passed a law in 1962 declaring six adjacent communities to be Flemish, no matter how many French-language families settle in those suburbs. French-speaking people call the law "a yoke"; Flemings say it is an attempt to prevent further growth of the "stain which must not spread."

No country in Europe has so complicated a school system. Not only does the government maintain what we would call public schools, it also pays most of the cost for private, largely religious, elementary and secondary education. In Flanders, classes go on in Dutch, with French offered as a second language. In Wallonia, French teaching prevails, but many pupils choose English or German as their second language. Add to this tangle the fact that in the small German culture region, lessons are conducted in German. Schooling is compulsory from age six to fourteen, but young people wishing to continue may stay in school until eighteen. Boys from twelve to eighteen attend a high school called an *athénée* (atheneum); girls go to a *lycée*. Today coeducation is becoming more general.

About two out of three newspapers are printed in French, although the actual circulation of Flemish printed papers is as large. One German daily comes out, while Antwerp publishes a paper in all three national tongues. Belgians read the news, for

2.5 million copies go out every day to the 9.5 million people.
Radio broadcasts come from separate French and Flemish stations, with the American armed forces station broadcasting news
in English. Radio music ranges from Beethoven to the Beatles.
Nine different television channels come on in early afternoon and
carry through the evening; two are national, one broadcasting in
French and the other in Dutch. Of the seven others two emanate
from Holland, two from France, two from Germany, and one
from the Grand Duchy of Luxembourg.

Although even moderates acknowledge the seriousness of the
language-culture division, they are aware that many interests
hold Belgians together: hardships endured in the past, a predomi-
nant religious faith (despite constitutional freedom of worship,
the population is largely Roman Catholic, although there are several Protestant denominations and a small Jewish community).
They repeat that, above all, the nation unites in wanting economic progress and diplomatic prestige. Few Flemings speak of
union with Holland. Nevertheless, a strong party has fought for
division into loosely federated sections, and, indeed, in 1968
began a parliamentary debate which ended in the most drastic
amendment to the constitution since it was drawn up in 1831. In
1970, parliament agreed to decentralize much administrative authority. Councils in each of the four linguistic regions—the Flemish area, the Walloon region, the bilingual Brussels area, and the
eastern German-speaking sector—manage cultural, economic, and
educational affairs. There is still a central government over all,
and continuity of institutions and interests guarantees the nation's unity.

3

The Air of the Town
Makes a Man Free

Flying over Belgium, you see it as a green, black, and silver fabric netted by rivers, canals, railroads, and highways, embroidered thickly with villages, spotted by mines, quarries, and smelters. When you think of the many and varied Belgian industries and recall that more people live here to the square mile than anywhere else in Europe except Holland, you find such words as rich, crowded, complicated to describe the land below you.

Belgian history, too, is rich and crowded. It is complicated by princely intrigues, claims to rulership based on royal marriages, ambition for land and power, commercial rivalries between cities and between nations, religious hatreds. Over the past thousand years, most of the wars of western Europe have raged across Flanders and Wallonia.

Yet, through the turmoil, the inhabitants of the region have kept their dreams of independence. Because they were not free, they valued freedom above everything else. Revolting again and again at the tyranny of their lords and the oppression of invaders, men died for liberty. Citizen rebellions were crushed, but gradually the rulers yielded a share of local self-government to the hardy, determined people. In the Middle Ages, men said, "The air of the town makes a man free," and it is true that the united strength of the townsmen won the first small rights to a share in local affairs.

The idea of self-government was born early in the Netherlands, as the area comprising both Belgium and Holland was called. Netherlands towns prospered in the dim past. They grew along Roman roads or on navigable rivers near the sea, and their merchants, craftsmen, and other workers built up a lively trade at home and abroad. As towns became larger, the citizens banded together according to their occupations into guilds or corporations: there was a bakers' guild; the weavers had a guild; the brewers formed a guild. Some cities counted as many as fifty-two different corporations, which regulated hours and working conditions for members, fixed pay and length of apprenticeship for those learning the trade, and fought for a voice in choosing town officials, in fixing taxes, and in determining when the citizens should be called for military service.

The Crusades, which began at the end of the eleventh century, helped the towns and strengthened the guilds. Belgian princes, who flocked to rescue Jerusalem and the Holy Sepulcher from the Saracens, took armies of their followers with them, and to raise enormous sums needed to finance the long and costly expeditions, they not only disposed of lands and castles but also sold rights and privileges to towns on their estates.

The merchants and tradesmen often paid well for the lord's written promise never again to collect a certain heavy tax. They bought his permission to build a wall about their town so as to defend it better. They bargained for the right to raise a high bell tower. The burghers of the Netherlands considered a belfry as the symbol of liberty and thought whoever held the tower ruled the town. A city's charter of rights and all its valuable documents could be locked away behind the iron doors of a room at the base of the tower. The bells above, which warned of fire, flood, and

A nineteenth-century statue of Godfrey of Bouillon, who led the First Crusade in the eleventh century.

the approach of enemies, and which summoned citizens to the public square to hear good news or bad, were the city's voices of anger, grief, and joy.

The Latin inscription on one old bell reads: "I praise the true God; I summon the people; I assemble the clergy; I mourn the dead; I put the plague to flight; I wail at the funeral; I abate the lightning; I proclaim the Sabbath; I arouse the lazy; I scatter the winds; I soften the cruel." If the people believed all these claims, they though the bell had magical powers. Of course we do not know exactly what they did believe, but we are certain they regarded their bells with pride and affection; indeed, they still do.

They gave names to the mighty ones—Roeland was the big bell of Ghent; Karolus and Gabriel lorded it over the smaller bells in Antwerp.

As the towns bought and fought themselves free of the nobles, you might expect to hear they were governed in a democratic way. Usually, this was not true. When some burghers, like the merchants and brewers, for example, grew richer and more important than their fellow citizens, they assumed more than their share of authority. Powerful guilds, ignoring poorer corporations, refused them a voice in city affairs. Sometimes this attitude brought on civil war between the arrogant rich and the truculent poor. More than once, Ghent, Bruges, Ieper (Ypres), and other cities saw their own men cut one another's throats in class fighting.

The most famous quarrel of this kind developed into a thrilling story which ended with the Battle of the Golden Spurs, so well described in Hendrik Conscience's novel, *The Lion of Flanders*. When the aristocrats of Bruges became too overbearing, the count of Flanders sided with the poorer people against them. Enraged, the aristocrats turned for support to King Philip the Fair of France. The French king was delighted at an excuse for meddling in Flemish affairs and sent armed help to the *Leliaerts*, or Men of the Lily, as the king's party called themselves because of the lily on the banners of France. The workers, on the other hand, rallied about the count of Flanders, calling themselves the *Clauwaerts*, or Men of the Lion's Claw, from the lion on their lord's coat of arms.

Philip invaded Flanders, defeated the Clauwaerts, took the count prisoner and raised the French fleur-de-lis over Bruges where the lion's banner had lately waved; he believed he had won the city. But he did not know how to deal with his new subjects, for he immediately levied new taxes. The Flemish detested (and still detest) taxes of all kinds. To make things worse, he garrisoned the town with French soldiers whose insolence infuriated the citizens.

Now, when the French entered Bruges, they had failed to capture five thousand of the principal Clauwaerts, who had fled to nearby towns and farms. As discontent grew within the city and news spread abroad that it was ready to revolt, a son of the count of Flanders plotted its delivery with two of the escaped Clauwaerts leaders, Pieter de Coninc, a weaver, and the butcher, Jan Breydel. We hear little about Jan, but a great deal about Pieter, who, though a frail and sickly man with only one eye, was a born leader able to inspire his comrades with his own courage.

Just before dawn one summer morning, he led the Clauwaerts back into Bruges through breaches the French had made in the city walls. Inside the city, they were joined by Clauwaerts sympathizers. The combined force struck suddenly and savagely. They fell upon the French. Any man who could not say "shield and friend" in Flemish with a Flemish accent was considered a Frenchman and killed without mercy. This slaughter is known as the Matins of Bruges, because it took place early in the morning —too pretty a name for such an ugly dawn.

When word of the Matins reached King Philip, he swore revenge and began gathering together an army of his best knights. The Clauwaerts were not frightened, nor did they shrink from the battle they knew must be fought. Instead, they appealed to all the neighboring towns for help. Ieper sent twelve hundred men, "five hundred dressed in scarlet, seven hundred dressed in black"; seven hundred managed to leave Ghent, while other volunteers came from as far away as Liège. On July 11, 1302, near Kortrijk (Courtrai) south of Bruges, the Clauwaerts and their allies met the splendor of Philip's chivalry.

What happened was almost unbelievable. The Clauwaerts were

on foot except for some thirty mounted knights attending the son of the count of Flanders. Philip's army consisted of superbly armed horsemen reinforced by a body of crossbowmen from Genoa in Italy. The Clauwaerts wore no armor except iron helmets; they carried heavy pikes as their only weapons. Yet they held against the French onslaught, standing with pikes fixed firm as an iron wall. The French charge, having been too hasty, broke against the pikes, and the horses scattered and stumbled in the marshy earth, dragging down their heavily armored riders. Seeing the confusion, the Flemish rushed upon the enemy and killed without quarter. When the battle was over, de Coninc's soldiers took seven hundred pairs of golden spurs from the feet of knights lying dead on the field. They gave the spurs to the church of Onze Lieve Vrouw in Kortrijk, where they hung for many years. You may visit this church in Kortrijk, for it has survived wars that destroyed so much else in the city, but you look in vain for the golden spurs, and no one can tell you what became of them.

It is a shame the story of this victory does not end: "And Flanders lived happy ever after." However, as history rarely works out so neatly, the best we can say here is: "After Kortrijk, Flanders kept the French at bay for twenty years." Then France prevailed and the Flemish took up their hard struggle for independence. Soon the Netherlands was involved in the Hundred Years' War between France and England.

England was Flanders' friend. If you look at the map, you see why. London, on the Thames, lies directly across the North Sea from the mouth of the Scheldt. For centuries, trade with inland Europe, flowing through the Netherlands by river, canal, and road to port cities like Bruges, came on over the narrow strip of sea to London. The English realized that safe, open Flemish ports favored their own commerce; that their prosperity depended on the thousands of pounds of English wool which the Flemish weavers bought and made into cloth so fine in texture and quality it was sold as far away as Russia and Denmark. For their part, the Flemish saw their best hope of shaking off French rule in help from this neighbor and business associate which also hated France.

Nevertheless, when King Edward III of England claimed the French throne in 1340, the people of Flanders tried to remain neutral in the Hundred Years' War brought on by his demands. The king of France agreed to respect their neutrality—and then immediately broke his promise. Realizing they must take sides, the Flemish followed the lead of Jacob van Artevelde, an influential merchant of Ghent, who offered his city's help to the English king. Edward came to Flanders—in Ghent you can see the ruins of Sint Baafs Monastery, where he lived while plotting his campaign against the French.

At first, Edward's plans went well. Leading his fleet of three hundred vessels in a raid up the River Zwyn, he attacked eight hundred French ships anchored off the town of Sluis and won a smashing victory. Today, you can go over that battle site without walking on water, for Sluis, just across the Belgian frontier in Holland, is now an inland town! In the century after Edward's victory, tides so completely silted up the Zwyn that polder fields replaced sea water about Sluis. Deep, deep down in polder mud lie rotted ship hulks, and rust that used to be weapons. If you could dig far enough, perhaps you might find gold and silver coins, sailors' medals and charms, even a gold chain or ring or a jeweled sword hilt embedded in the silt.

Sluis was the only British success in so many years that Flanders lost heart and King Edward went home to England. In Ghent, van Artevelde's enemies turned on him and murdered him. Flanders's share of the Hundred Years' War proved to be destruction, disease, and death.

The war brought ruin of another kind, because when Edward left, some of the best Flemish weavers followed him to England, where they taught their craft to the English, who thereafter made their own wool into cloth, while the weavers in Flanders had to buy Spanish wool, a product so harsh and inferior that all the Flemish skill could not turn it into the fine material of earlier days. Gradually, England captured the woolen goods trade in Europe, and cities like Ghent, Ieper, Kortrijk had to begin making linen from the flax which grew, and still grows, in fields about Kortrijk. However, in the Kempen region, the textile cities did not find any industry to substitute. The looms stood idle. Weavers and dyers drifted away in search of work. And the towns dwindled into the villages we see today, each huddled about a church too large and handsome for such an insignificant place.

4

The Grand Dukes of the West

Bruges, Ghent, and the other Flanders cities were not the only ones to struggle for liberty and power. Although Flanders developed earlier than the rest of the country, the history of most of the Netherlands tells of towns growing rich and self-reliant, burghers wresting individual liberty from their overlords and poor workers fighting for and winning equality with the important citizens. Only in the Ardennes was the story different, because the Ardennes, with few towns, peasants living like serfs among the forests, and robber lords in fortress castles, seemed centuries behind the times.

By the middle of the fourteenth century, not only were the inhabitants of the province of Brabant protected by charters guaranteeing their rights and privileges, but they were also busy and successful. The city of Brussels, though not so splendid as Bruges or Ghent, flourished. Brussels-made armor glinted in tournaments throughout Europe; Brussels tapestry hung in castles from Scandinavia to Spain; kings, princes, churches bought the work of Brussels gold and silversmiths.

Dinant, one of "the twenty-two good towns" of the bishopric of Liège, was making fine beaten brass and copper vessels as early as the tenth century. Verviers, another of the good towns, wove tex-

Dinant, on the Meuse River, with its thirteenth-century church on the right.

tiles by 1300—it is still an important woolen-mill town. Artisans and craftsmen of the city of Liège turned out handsome weapons and forged iron objects. Today the guns and locomotives manufactured in Liège are a great source of Belgian riches.

Even before the Battle of the Golden Spurs, the workers of Liège had forced from the bishop who was their ruling prince the right to join churchmen and nobles in making laws and fixing taxes for the province. They kept this privilege by fighting the nobles as well as the bishop, and year after year, class struggles tore the city with murders, revenges, wholesale massacres, and the destruction of property. Then in the fifteenth century the artisans and nobles faced a common enemy—the dukes of Burgundy, who, absorbing the Netherlands through marriage, military conquests, and the purchase of territory, hoped to weld their lands into a monarchy. They called themselves the Grand Dukes of the West, but dreamed of being kings of the heartland of Europe. Their ruthlessness and cruelty almost achieved this ambition, because they did not hesitate to do away with local privileges or use force to gain more power for themselves. When Ghent and Bruges rebelled at interference in city matters by Duke Philip the Good, he besieged both cities and executed the leaders of the uprisings. When Dinant rebelled in the last years of his reign, his son Charles the Bold sacked and burned the place, destroyed its town hall and cathedral, and ordered eight hundred citizens, tied together in pairs, drowned in the Meuse.

The story of Liège is more savage yet. If you have read Sir Walter Scott's novel, *Quentin Durward,* or seen the movie based on it, you remember how wily King Louis XI of France distrusted Charles the Bold, who was his vassal. Charles, for his part, loathed doing homage to Louis, and longed to be a king, too, and independent. The Liégeois also feared and hated Charles for his meddling in their affairs. Liège had been free as Burgundy for five hundred years; where Burgundy owed allegiance to France, Liège paid homage to the German emperor. Nevertheless, Charles was determined to annex the province.

Seeing a chance to turn Charles's quarrel with Liège to his own advantage, King Louis sent undercover agents to the people with promises of money and arms if they would defy the duke. The Liégeois attempted several small uprisings, for which Charles punished them severely. Then they attacked the bishop, Charles' cousin, who had been forced on them by the Burgundians. But their timing was bad—they chose the very moment when Louis happened to be visiting Charles in his castle of Peronne. When news of the fracas, in which the bishop had not been hurt, reached Peronne, along with information about Louis's trouble-making, Charles told his royal guest he was a prisoner and would remain so until he agreed to join an expedition against Liège. Louis quickly agreed.

News of the approaching French-Burgundian army sent the chief citizens of Liège and the leading rebels scurrying into the Ardennes, leaving behind the poor, the old, and women and children in hopes the duke would spare them as harmless. The bishop himself rode out to meet his cousin and the king to beg mercy for the city, but they would not listen to him. Once inside Liège, Charles ordered its inhabitants killed, so many a day, and the city looted, then destroyed so much of it every day. About fifty thousand Liégeois died in their ruined homes or were thrown into the Meuse to drown, while all buildings except churches were burned or torn down. Even in the brutal fifteenth century, the fate of Liège shocked Europe.

Yet in spite of such instances of tyranny and cruelty, Burgundian rule is the glory of early Netherlands history. For the first time, the country was almost united; never had it been more respected abroad, or richer. All Europe bought its textiles, tapestry, lace, weapons, gold and enamel wares, beaten copper, forged iron. Ships sailing up the River Zwyn unloaded on the wharves of Damme, the port of Bruges, cargoes of English tin, lead, and cheese, German wine, Spanish and Portuguese figs, olives, or-

The 407 steps of Bueren Mountain commemorate Vincent de Bueren, who attempted to defend Liège against the French and Burgundians.

anges, and lemons. Cloth of gold came from Italy, furs from Russia, rugs from the Middle East, horses from Denmark, lions, monkeys, and parrots from Africa. Merchants and bankers from seventeen foreign countries lived in Bruges in homes luxurious as palaces. The feasts and pageants of the nobles and rich merchants made society news for all Europe.

The dukes of Burgundy kept more splendid state than any kings. Their court shone with storybook chivalry. In 1429, to commemorate his marriage with the Portuguese princess Isabella, Philip the Good founded the Order of the Golden Fleece, which somewhat resembles the Order of the Garter, established a hundred years earlier by King Edward III of England. For centuries afterwards, kings and princes of Europe coveted the honor of being a Knight of the Golden Fleece and proudly wore its jewel-studded golden chain or broad red ribbon, from which hung a small golden figure of a sheep.

In Brussels the Grand'Place is a vast public square laid out in Burgundian times as a site for tournaments. Hundreds of armed knights have jousted there to honor a ducal wedding or the birth of a duke's child. The figure of Saint Michael glitters from the spire of the Brussels town hall; spire and Saint Michael rose up from the Grand'Place into the sky during the reign of Philip the Good.

His reign was the beginning of an age when religious orders, nobles, guilds, and rich tradesmen vied with each other in building monasteries, churches, mansions, and town halls; but beyond all the others, Philip, and after him his son Charles, lavished wealth and honors on artists. The dukes commissioned buildings, statues, paintings, gold and silver work; they ordered costumes designed, scenery and decorations made for the pageants which marked every Burgundian festival. It seems natural that Flemish painting should flower in Philip's reign, and proper to associate the last two great dukes, Philip and Charles, with the Flemish painters who, immortalizing the quiet Flanders landscape and the faces and figures of their fellow citizens, produced some of the world's masterpieces.

Duke Philip sent the painter Jan van Eyck to Portugal with the diplomats who arranged the duke's marriage to the Princess Isabella. It is probable that the artist's portrait of the lady gave Philip his first idea of what she looked like. You see van Eyck's work in Antwerp, Bruges, and Ghent, but particularly in Ghent, where a small chapel of Sint Baafs Cathedral contains the *Adoration of the Mystic Lamb,* considered one of the five or six greatest pictures in existence. Jan's shadowy brother Hubert is supposed to have begun the painting, but Jan, the younger by twenty years,

finished it after Hubert's death. This multipaneled altarpiece has
gone through a series of mystery-story adventures, for sections of
it have been stolen more than once, only to be recovered. Only
one panel has completely disappeared. Napoleon's soldiers carried
off the central panel to Paris, where it hung in the Louvre until
his downfall. Thieves made away with six sidepieces that were
sold and resold until finally the king of Prussia bought them for
the Berlin Art Gallery. The peace treaty signed after World War
I provided for their return to Ghent. When World War II threat-
ened, the Belgian government sent the altarpiece to southern
France for safety. However, when France fell, the Vichy regime
gave the painting to the Nazis, although there was no need to do
so, since it was in the unoccupied part of France. The Nazis took
it off to Germany and after the war it turned up with other missing art treasures in a salt mine in Austria. Now, with one original
panel missing, it has come home to Sint Baafs. A panel has been
substituted for the lost original and only an art expert would
know it is not genuine.

You need not try to interpret the religious meaning of the
work to enjoy its beauty, but you will have a hard time believing
that the graceful figures and the enchanting backgrounds were
painted five hundred years ago, so fresh and brilliant are the
colors.

Although German-born, Hans Memling is considered a Flemish master, because he lived and worked most of his life in
Bruges. Like van Eyck, Memling portrayed people and scenes
with childlike, yet realistic clarity. His colors, too, have kept their
freshness. However, he surpasses van Eyck and the other artists of
his time in religious feeling and imagination, in his gift for en-
chantment. Memling's greatest works are in Saint John's Hospital
in Bruges. Among them is a portrait of Martin Nieuwenhoven,
who seems to have been an important burgher of the town,

though far from its handsomest. Martin's nose is big, his features heavy, and the bluish-gray velvet and wool suit he wears emphasizes the sallowness of his complexion. You would not say that he has an interesting face, and yet, as he prays, he really looks as though he sees a vision—the vision of the Madonna painted as a companion work to his portrait. The picture of Martin Nieuwenhoven is not Memling's masterpiece, but it shows how he could mirror a man's soul.

Rogier van der Weyden, a third artist of the Flemish school, was a Walloon who lived in Bruges (where he was Memling's teacher) and later settled in Brussels. As the painters he worked with were Flemish, he translated his French name, Roger de la Pasture, into its Flemish equivalent and became Rogier van der Weyden. In his religious pictures, the Blessed Virgin and the saints look like dignified Netherlanders posed against rich tapestries near stained-glass windows opening on Netherlandish scenery—river or canal, battlements, turrets, and gabled roofs. One feels their human quality more than their saintliness.

Van der Weyden also painted the great men of his day, among others Philip the Good and Charles the Bold, and these portraits are priceless character sketches. When you see Charles as the artist saw him, you understand the fears of King Louis and the hatred of Liège. How arrogantly Charles wears the chain of the Golden Fleece! He holds his sword hilt with long, stiff fingers and glares at you with scorn. Gazing at him, you recall how his impatience and harshness undid all his father had accomplished toward uniting the Netherlands; you believe he loved war for its own sake, and feel a foreshadowing of his terrible fate. He fell in a winter battle before Nancy in France and when, days later, his followers found his body among the dead, it had been half devoured by wolves.

Charles's daughter Mary inherited the duchy at nineteen. With enemies harrying her on every side, she quickly married the man she thought best able to defend her lands, a German prince named Maximilian. Later on, Maximilian became an emperor, ruler of the Holy Roman Empire, a confederation of European states, but he could not keep peace with the Netherlands cities or with France, especially after Mary's death a few years following her marriage. The greatness of the Netherlands was over; less than half a century after the death of Charles the Bold, it became a Spanish possession when it was inherited by another Charles, the grandson of Mary and Maximilian.

This Charles acquired the throne of Spain through his mother's parents, King Ferdinand and Queen Isabella. The Netherlands came to him from his father, the son of Mary and Maximilian. Born in Ghent and brought up in the city of Mechelen, Charles preferred his native land to his mother's country when he was young, but as he grew older he took more interest in Spain and in the affairs of the empire, where he succeeded Maximilian as ruler. He is usually called Charles V because he was the fifth emperor of the name. As the years went by, the Spaniards almost forgave him for being a "foreigner," but his popularity faded in the Netherlands. His own city of Ghent revolted against him and later on even replaced his statue with one to the murdered Jacob van Artevelde.

Charles was ostentatious like his Burgundian ancestors. He also had his great-grandfather Charles's passion for war, wasting much of his life and too much of his people's resources on the Burgundian feud with France. Endless campaigns and a restless life made him old by the time he was fifty-five. Knowing he had not long to live, he came back from Spain, thin as a skeleton, dressed in mourning black, and in a simple ceremony in the royal palace on the hill above Brussels turned over rule of the Netherlands to his son Philip.

5

The Spanish Netherlands Becomes Belgium

While the Netherlands chafed under the rule of Charles V, the country had even more cause for discontent under his son Philip II, because Philip thought only of Spain and treated the Netherlanders like conquered people. Charles's wars had dragged them deep into debt. Philip demanded still more taxes for further wars. Charles had curbed the independence of several cities, but Philip's policy was to destroy all individual liberty and gather power to himself.

Charles set up the Inquisition in the Netherlands. Philip kept the Inquisitors busy. The Protestant Reformation, as it spread through the Netherlands, had made converts in both the northern and southern provinces. Philip believed the Inquisition could drive these converts back into the Catholic Church or so punish them as to frighten others away from the new faith. He urged and encouraged the Inquisitors to try anyone suspected of differing in thought, word, or deed from Catholic teachings. As a result, thousands of men and women were condemned to heavy punishment or death for their beliefs.

Philip underestimated the independent spirit of the Netherlands, for Protestantism continued to grow. Thousands of converts fled to England, Germany, Sweden, but even more remained

45

at home to riot and rebel against oppression. They wrecked
churches and convents, smashed statues and stained glass, burned
wood carvings, slashed and burned paintings. Philip's reply to
their fierce disobedience was just as fierce. He sent the Duke of
Alva from Spain to restore order. Alva, a ruthless soldier, brought
bloodshed and horror to the country. Sometimes his soldiers mas-
sacred the inhabitants of an entire village in reprisal for an attack
on a Spanish soldier. His court, called the Council of Blood, tried
and sentenced to death on the least pretext. Men were hanged for
failure to pay exorbitant taxes.

Such brutality brought on rebellion and then plunged the
country into open civil war. The leader of the opposition was
Prince William of Orange, a nobleman who had been devoted to
Charles V. At first, Prince William may not have planned to
shake off Spanish rule, but may have hoped, rather, to make
Philip behave with more humanity and justice, and in this move-
ment he had the support of all the Netherlanders. However, religious disputes soon divided his followers. In the north, which had
become solidly Protestant, people refused to let their Catholic allies worship in their territory, while those inhabitants who chose
to remain in the southern provinces were just as stubbornly Catholic. When William declared himself a Protestant about twelve
years after the outbreak of war, his Catholic followers in the south
gave up the fight and accepted Philip's offer to soften his policies.
The seven provinces of the Protestant north, however, refused to
make peace with the king and fought on. Their struggle lasted for
thirty more years until, at last, in the early seventeenth century,
they were recognized as the free nation of Holland.

The Southern Netherlands, that is, the area corresponding to
modern Belgium, waited two hundred years before achieving independence. For half of that time, it remained a Spanish possession. Considering Spain's long occupation, Belgium shows surpris-

ingly few Spanish traits. Houses with dark, Spanish-tiled roofs can be seen in Brussels and Antwerp and at Veurne (Furnes) in Flanders, the most Spanish of all Belgian towns. Some Belgians have dark Spanish eyes, shining black hair, and finely chiseled features. One or two customs exist that may perhaps be traced back to Spanish times. That is all, except for several festivals, notably the carnival at Binche and the Procession of the Penitents at Veurne.

Binche has gone mad at carnival time ever since 1549, when Charles V happened to be visiting his sister at her castle in the town. She arranged a celebration in honor of the recent Spanish conquest of Peru. The plumes and gaudy costumes of the *Gilles* (players) of Binche are supposed to make the wearers look like the Incas of Peru. Every man in the town aspires to be a Gille, a member of the association which stages the carnival; every small boy longs to wear one day their heavily padded, embroidered costume with a cap from which tower ostrich plumes, to walk to the jingling of bells sewed on his suit.

The Gilles take over Binche for three days beginning on the Sunday before Mardi Gras and ending as Lent dawns. They parade down streets hung with red and yellow Spanish flags and littered with red and yellow confetti trailing from upper windows. Lower windows of shops and houses along the line of march have been boarded up against the barrage of oranges which the Gilles throw as they go, oranges that flatten on house fronts, spatter the streets, and plop against the bodies of unlucky spectators. Yet this golden threat is forgotten in the excitement of hurdy-gurdy and viola music, the rhythm of wooden shoes click-clacking on the cobbles, the smell of bonfires sharp in the winter air. When the final procession reaches the Main Square on Mardi Gras evening, paraders and spectators circle in a wild dance. Later on come fireworks; still later, the Gilles and their guests dance at a masked ball. No wonder the Carnival at Binche is supposed to have given us our slang term "binge."

The Procession of the Penitents at Veurne is a different affair. Its floats depicting religious scenes, its marchers acting out Bible stories as they go by, and especially the penitents recall gloomy medieval ideas of sin and atonement. Some of these black-robed penitents, their heads and faces swathed in black hoods, walk

Gilles of Binche.

barefoot over the cobbles, each carrying a heavy cross in repentance for some sin he has committed. The lovely Spanish town hall of Veurne, the houses with blue- and red-tiled roofs have witnessed this show for three hundred years. The spectacle lends an air of chilling reality, a sense of the past. However, no sooner does the last parader disappear than the crowds forget the awe with which they have watched, and begin milling around booths of a fair set up in the marketplace. The gloomy mood has gone; a spectator scarcely believes that only a little while ago a drama of grief and repentance was being played out instead of a carnival scene.

Perhaps Belgium shows so little Spanish influence because comparatively few Spaniards came to the Netherlands. Instead, the armies Spain sent into the country comprised Italians, Germans, French, and other Europeans hired to fight in Europe while Spaniards themselves went off to explore, exploit, and colonize the New World. These hired soldiers were often disreputable fellows who drank, robbed, bullied, and were hated and avoided wherever they went. King Philip's promise to withdraw them was one concession which helped to pacify the southern Netherlands.

Almost immediately after Philip's death, his daughter, Archduchess Isabella, and her husband, Archduke Albert, came to rule the southern Netherlands. The people liked Isabella, so merry and kindhearted, so unlike her somber father and they respected the thin, serious Albert's efforts to govern justly. This couple brought with them the happiest years, the most nearly peaceful time the Spanish Netherlands had known.

If Albert and Isabella had had a son to inherit the throne the Spanish Netherlands might have been a happier land. However, they were childless. When Albert died in 1621, the southern Netherlands reverted to the king of Spain. Isabella survived her husband by twelve years, but she acted merely as regent. By the middle of the seventeenth century, the country plunged again into Spain's wars with France, England, and Holland. Enemy soldiers trampled fields, pillaged and damaged villages and towns. If one knows the names of famous European battles of the age, one can find many of them on the map of Belgium and understand what an Englishman meant when he wrote, "The Netherlands have been the very cockpit of Christendom." (The term "cockpit" means a spot where fighting cocks spur and peck each other to death.)

At the beginning of the eighteenth century, a French prince and an Austrian archduke fought for the Spanish throne, which had been left vacant by the death of the last direct heir. At this war's end the archduke had lost Spain, but he kept the Spanish Netherlands as a consolation prize. Austria ruled for eighty years, during which the land did not fare too badly. Nevertheless, the end of the century found the inhabitants restless and dissatisfied.

Revolution was the political fashion of the day. The United States had lately won independence from England. The French Revolution was shaking Europe. Clouds of discontent, drifting across the European continent, hung over the southern Netherlands. When the well-meaning Emperor Joseph II of Austria tried to tell his "new" subjects how to live, they resented his interference. When he wanted to change the way in which Catholic priests were educated, the storm burst. Imitating Americans and Frenchmen, rebellious Belgians drove out the Austrians and declared a United States of Belgium. But the young republic was too feeble to last; within a few months its leaders were quarreling among themselves, while the great powers, England, France, Prussia, and of course, Austria, ordered the nation reunited with Austria. The United States of Belgium had lasted through the year 1790, then it dissolved into the Austrian Netherlands. But Austria did not rule much longer. Soon, troops of the French revolutionary government, which was at war with Austria, swarmed in. By 1793, Austria had lost the southern Netherlands to France. Now, for the first time since Burgundian days, the province of Liège joined the other provinces. The Liégeois, who had so bitterly resisted Charles the Bold of Burgundy in the fifteenth century, welcomed French rule in the eighteenth, because they admired the ideals proclaimed by the revolution and hoped to enjoy that "Liberty, Equality and Fraternity" promised by the revolutionary slogan.

Liège and the rest of Belgium soon learned how little liberty or equality French rule brought. They groaned under high taxes and obeyed harsh, corrupt officials. French soldiers looted like enemy troops. Citizens were conscripted for service in the French army. "Defenders" of Liberty, Equality and Fraternity closed churches, desecrated some, and tore down others; they persecuted priests and mocked at religion. Not surprisingly, citizens revolted again. The uprising came in country districts, where peasants armed with scythes, old guns, and rusty pikes fought French regulars. Such an unequal contest did not last long; the rebels were soon defeated and their leaders executed.

When Napoleon Bonaparte assumed supreme power, he corrected some abuses and restored a measure of freedom. With his mania for improving and building, he tore down the city walls around Brussels, marking their traces by wide boulevards. Belgium seems to be the one country in Europe outside of France where he is not universally detested. Flemings and Walloons enlisted in his armies; some even became soldiers of his famous Old Guard. Others, however, fought under the British general, the Duke of Wellington, when in 1815, England, Holland, and Prussia put an end to Napoleon's career by defeating him at the Battle of Waterloo, fought a few miles south of Brussels.

After Waterloo, the victors, having packed Napoleon off to exile

The battlefield of Waterloo. In the foreground are museums and the Waterloo Mound, a monument commemorating Napoleon's defeat.

on the Island of Saint Helena in the South Atlantic, began to rearrange the map of Europe, which he had changed to suit himself. They evidently considered the southern Netherlands as part of the spoils of war and, without consulting the people, joined the land to Holland in a kingdom called the United Netherlands. In thus forming a single nation they hoped to establish a state large enough and strong enough to block French aggression in the future. They were not concerned about putting together two halves which did not make a whole. Nor did they recall that, after more than two centuries of separation, the northern and southern Netherlanders had no love for each other. The Protestant Dutch distrusted the Catholic Belgians, who hated them. Almost the only benefit of the so-called union was that the port of Antwerp, long closed by Dutch control of the Scheldt, reopened to traffic.

A ruler diplomatic enough to ease tensions between north and south might have united them, but William I, who had ruled Holland as Prince of Orange before becoming king of the United Netherlands, was neither farseeing nor tactful, even though he tried to improve the economic state of the nation. He did not hide his contempt for the Catholic religion of his new subjects. Indeed he refused to hear their complaints about injustices, real or imagined. He even suppressed newspapers and punished journalists reporting the discontent. Belgians did not share equally in government with Hollanders as they had been promised, but sent fewer representatives to parliament in proportion to population, while almost all cabinet ministers, diplomats, and army officers were Dutch. Since public office was open only to Dutch-speaking applicants, this often excluded Flemish as well as Walloons, for at the time most educated Flemings spoke French and, at best, knew only some corrupt Flemish dialect.

Both Flanders and Wallonia resented William's severity and grudged Holland its lion's share of power. Bad feeling grew with the years until, in 1830, the southern provinces revolted. By prearranged plan, the uprising began with a riot during a performance being given in the Brussels opera house, the Théâtre de la Monnaie. King William sent his second son with an army to put down the trouble. (His older son is said to have refused to fight Belgians, whom he preferred to the Dutch.) After three days of skirmishing, Dutch forces withdrew from the capital. Within

three weeks, William had lost all the south except for forts at
Antwerp and Maastricht, a city on the Meuse. Eventually, defenders of Antwerp's citadel surrendered, but Maastricht held. It
remains Dutch to this day.

The revolutionists declared an independent nation and named
it Belgium. At last, the term so often used in the nineteenth century became official. From this time on, only Holland was known
as the Netherlands. The Belgians invited Prince Leopold of

A view of Antwerp and the Scheldt River, which makes the city an
international seaport.

Saxe-Coburg to be their first king, a choice which England approved, since Leopold, though German-born, was a naturalized British subject. France became a second powerful friend upon Leopold's marriage to the daughter of its king. Without the political support of England and actual French military aid against Dutch attempts to retake the territory, Belgium might not have survived the hard early years. Finally Holland admitted that the new nation belonged on the map and in 1839 France, Russia, Prussia, and Austria, meeting with the British in London, recognized an independent nation of Belgium, at the same time directing it to remain perpetually neutral. This meant it could not take sides in any European conflict. Each of the five powers promised not merely to respect this neutrality, but also to defend the land against invaders.

After the Belgian-Dutch split, the latter again closed the Scheldt to traffic to Antwerp, and Antwerp died again until negotiations finally reopened it. Today, not only Antwerp but Ghent also, which is farther inland on the river, are flourishing seaports.

6

A Colony Eighty Times as Big

Because Leopold I entered Brussels as king on July 21, 1831, the anniversary of this occasion remains a national holiday, observed by church services, parades, sports contests, carillon concerts, and brilliantly lighted streets and fireworks at night. The nation could not celebrate a more suitable day than the twenty-first of July for Leopold's reign began the best era in ten centuries. The king proved to be cautious, wise, and tactful at home, a diplomat abroad. He ruled under a constitution guaranteeing freedom of worship, free education, and a free press. Without him, this document might not have been strictly enforced. His influence strengthened the shaky young nation with such success that at his death in 1865 Belgium was united and prosperous at home, respected abroad.

His son Leopold II did just as much for the country, but his contribution was so different that at times it earned him abuse from abroad and small thanks from his subjects. Not until after he died did Belgians recognize what he had accomplished. In an age of colonialism, he dreamed of creating an empire. He imagined a Belgium swollen with riches from colonies, perhaps in China, the Philippines, or Morocco, or along the Nile. Nevertheless, none of these dreams became fact until he began to think of central Africa.

About this time, the man who could help realize his dreams came back home, after spending three years in the heart of Africa. This was the British-born, naturalized United States journalist, Henry Morton Stanley, who had headed a relief party organized by a New York City newspaper and led it into central Africa to look for the explorer-missionary, David Livingstone, lost in the wilderness. When, after months of perilous adventure, Stanley found Doctor Livingstone on the shores of Lake Tanganyika, his first words are supposed to have been the casual: "Doctor Livingstone, I presume."

Two years after this meeting with Livingstone (who preferred to remain in Africa), Stanley undertook another expedition into Africa in an effort to trace the course of a river—the Nile, he hoped—rising in Lake Tanganyika. Three years, thirty cataracts, and twenty-five hundred miles later, he reached the mouth of the Congo River. He had fought jungles, heat, disease, and the poisoned arrows of cannibal tribesmen and lost most of the companions who had begun the journey with him. Only incredible courage and good luck brought him out alive from the dangers of the largest unexplored area remaining in Africa.

When Stanley returned to Europe with tales of land along the Congo, Leopold persuaded him to enter his service, sending him back to continue explorations, to set up trading posts, and to make treaties with native chiefs. In this way, the king acquired thousands of miles of territory. By 1885, he controlled an expanse of over 900,000 square miles (Belgium covers 11,000 square miles), the new territory swelling inland like a blown-up balloon with its only access to the South Atlantic a twenty-five-mile strip of shore along the northern bank of the Congo.

The king not only lavished his personal fortune on developing this realm; he also bullied or wheedled millions of francs from the Belgian government to finance exploitation, build roads, buy

boats (the first steamer to navigate the Congo River was a Missis-
sippi riverboat). Trading stations sprang up in the wilds, white
men died by the hundreds from heat, disease, snake bite, skirmishes with hostile Africans. But always work continued: the
clearing of jungles, cutting of roads, creation of shelters for travelers, the establishment of settlements for traders and technicians.

Thousands of black workers died of forced labor and bad treat-
ment by white and black overseers. Cargoes of natural rubber,
shipments of ivory and copper began to flow out from the Congo,
but so did tales of cruelty that shocked Europe and horrified and
embarrassed the Belgians, who still insist that some reports were
invented or exaggerated by a sensationalist press. Certainly there
were abuses; yet, on the other hand, Leopold's representatives
tried to dry up the slave trade which Arabs and some black chief-
tains had been carrying on. Belgian officials fought to end canni-
balism; they enforced a kind of peace among warring Congolese,
who numbered more than two hundred different tribes. All the
same, the fact remains that in the latter part of the nineteenth
century the Congo was considered by Europeans a sort of earthly
hell, and a mortified Belgian government urged the king to turn
over to it the control he had promised in return for loans made
him. Yet Leopold clung to his possession, determined that this
land, eighty times the size of Belgium, should remain his personal
estate so long as he lived, to rule as he chose. Not until a year before his death did he cede the Congo Free State to Belgium.
Thereafter the country went by the name of Belgian Congo.

King Albert I, Leopold's nephew, who succeeded him in 1909,
helped to establish a humane and apparently intelligent rule in
the land. He went to the Congo, where he traveled through
hundreds of miles of forests and jungles, often on foot. He thus
knew what reforms were needed, and such changes were made.
Belgian statesmen also concerned themselves with the colony's

well-being. Belgium was less selfish than many nations in colonial administration. Much of the revenue from the Congo's fabulous mineral and agricultural wealth was reinvested there in hospitals, schools, and sports arenas; Belgians built thousands of miles of roads and improved agriculture. The Congolese who worked mines, gathered copra for palm oil, and tended coffee, tea, cotton, and rubber plantations received medical care and elementary schooling. Shortly before 1960, UNESCO (the United Nations Educational, Scientific and Cultural Organization, representing 135 nations), called the Congo the best-governed, best-fed, best-housed, and best-educated territory between Cairo and Capetown.

However, Belgium's Congo policy, though humane for its time, had serious flaws. Through the years, the Congolese themselves took no part in government—white settlers in the country could not vote either—and few, very few black Congolese had gone on to higher education, although two universities did exist in the country. They were not ready to govern themselves. Yet, a Congolese middle class, a small group of better-educated professional men and minor government officials, raised the cry for self-government at a time when demands for independence were being made in many African countries. The mass of the people echoed the slogan "Independence Now" with ever louder voices. Belgium did not try to silence them by force, but instead reluctantly yielded to their demands. On June 30, 1960, Baudouin I, by then the king in Belgium, went to Africa to relinquish officially all control over the former colony. Just beforehand, Belgium gave the Congo some $80 million as working capital, at the same time promising to leave technical experts in key industries to help train Congolese successors.

A "Treaty of Friendship, Assistance and Cooperation" was signed in Leopoldville, the capital city, now called Kinshasa. King Baudouin made a friendly speech wishing the new nation well. To this, the Congolese prime minister, Patrice Lumumba, is reported to have replied in an angry harangue: "We are no longer your monkeys." Someone in the crowd snatched the sword from Baudouin as he was about to give it to Lumumba as a token of friendship.

Although Lumumba is reported to have apologized for his insults, the reception in Kinshasa set the tone for what followed over the next five years. Within a few days strikes, riots, even open warfare erupted in six of the seven provinces. Congolese soldiers mutinied against Belgian officers, and murdered many of them as well as other officials and technicians still in the country. They abused and killed women and children, robbed, looted, burned, and fought each other. Bearing in mind that this nation comprises two hundred separate, often hostile tribes who speak three hundred different dialects, one can perhaps understand the turmoil.

Only Katanga, the seventh province remained orderly. Moïse Tshombe, its provincial governor, declared secession from the confusion and horror which overwhelmed the rest of the Congo.

Since its fabulous mineral wealth made Katanga the richest province, Tshombe's act meant the loss of revenue vital to the newly formed democratic republic. When the six other provinces could not defeat nor subdue the Katangese, the United Nations sent in a force of soldiers, mainly recruited from African member lands, to impose "unity." Reliable Neutral and Belgian witnesses state that the "unifying" troops behaved as barbarously in Katanga as Congolese mutineers had in the other provinces. White settlers and the remaining white soldiers fled or tried to flee across the border to neighboring Tanganyika or Uganda. Many others were killed. Moïse Tshombe, after a series of adventures and misfortunes, was imprisoned in Algeria where he died. Patrice Lumumba met a mysterious death in Katanga.

Five years passed in a frenzy of destruction and violence until 1965, when a Congolese officer seized control and brought order out of turmoil. General Joseph Mobotu not only pacified the land but, realizing its need for European help, turned to Belgium. Upon an invitation from the king he went to Brussels for "peace talks." Successful talks they were, too, for since then Belgium has given regular financial aid to its former colony. Baudouin and his wife, Queen Fabiola, returned Mobotu's visit in 1970. In the capital, Kinshasa, the king again signed a treaty of friendship. This visit differed from the earlier one. Now the royal pair was met with enthusiasm and admiration. They conferred with the heads of government and mingled with the crowds of people. One important Congolese official is said to have exclaimed, "A new tradition is born, to consider Belgium as a second fatherland for the Congolese, and the Congo as a second fatherland for the Belgians."

The Democratic Republic of the Congo has renamed itself with the intriguing word Zaire. One authority says the term is a translation from the Portuguese meaning "Land Across the River." Although the political situation in Zaire is not yet stabilized, well-known industrial companies from Europe and the United States have begun to invest in its incredibly rich land, building manufacturing plants, managing plantations, mining, and exporting.

7

Five Kings and Two Wars

Most Belgians trusted the 1839 Treaty of London and believed in its guarantees of their neutrality. After about eighty years of peace, World War I stunned them. Leopold II, who had been more farseeing than his people, felt war was possible between France and Germany. (In 1871 Prussia had united with the other German provinces into a single nation, Germany, with the king of Prussia as its emperor). Fearing such a war might involve Belgium, the king wanted his country ready to repel any invaders, but he preached preparedness to people who weren't listening. Only with the greatest difficulty did he persuade the government to put up forts at Namur and Liège on the Meuse and at Antwerp on the Scheldt. For a long time, too, his plea for universal military training of young men was unpopular. Parliament did not enact a measure providing for such a system until Leopold lay dying. He is said to have written his name for the last time when he signed the bill into law.

Although King Albert, who followed him in 1909, also urged the Belgians to arm, they felt too secure to sacrifice for self-defense. Even when war came between Germany and Austria on one side and France and Russia on the other, most Belgians hoped to remain neutral. They were dumbfounded when the German minister in Brussels demanded permission for his nation's troops to pass through Belgium en route to France, promising that the invasion would be peaceful if they met no resistance. The king and his government spurned the proposal, saying that Belgium would fight if entered. Two days later, on August 4, 1914, German forces crossed the frontier and advanced on Liège. The next day England, keeping its pledge as a signer of the Treaty of London, declared war on Germany.

King Albert went to the front to command the Belgian Army. He had fewer than one hundred thousand soldiers. His men lacked arms and ammunition though not courage and fighting spirit. The fort at Liège held out against fierce assaults for ten days, time precious to France and England as they made frantic preparations for war. Slowly, fighting steadily, the Belgians retreated across country to the Yser River in West Flanders. While they held along the Yser in October, King Albert ordered the dikes cut where the river flows into the sea near the city of Nieuwpoort. With the dikes down, water swirled through the breach, turning the polders into shallow lakes, deep enough, though, to stop the German advance.

The small patch of Flanders between the Yser and the French border, between the cities of Ieper and Nieuwpoort, constituted the only part of Belgium the enemy did not hold, even though they went on trying to take it. After four years of skirmishes, bombings, artillery attacks, Ieper and Nieuwpoort lay shattered but still free. When peace returned, the citizens of each town rebuilt. The thirteenth-century town hall and the cathedral of Ieper resemble the original structures which had been destroyed. Nieuwpoort replaced its lovely old church, among other buildings. However, what draws us to that sector of Belgium today is not these restorations of the distant past but rather memories of our own century, such reminders as the arch set into the medieval ramparts of Ieper and inscribed: ". . . in honor of the heroism of the British Army and in memory of the fifty-six thousand Tommies who fell in the Ieper salient."

During the war years, that is from 1914 to 1918, Belgians resisted, protested, and outwitted the German occupation forces. They forgot that they were Flemings and Walloons and fused into one people sharing griefs and hopes for liberation. Encouraged by the example of their leaders, they dared to show their patriotism. King Albert and Queen Elizabeth, his wife, remained with the broken army on free Belgian soil, living in a cottage at De Panne, a fishing village tucked into the dunes. Cardinal Mercier, head of the Catholic Church in Belgium, defied the Germans time and again, denouncing injustices. Adolph Max, burgomaster (mayor) of Brussels, defended his people against ever-growing oppression until at last he was sent to prison in Germany. German officials complained of Belgian "disobedience." They forgot that the descendants of southern Netherlanders were merely exercising an old talent for flouting the enemy. Perhaps the Germans had never heard what a French poet said of the country: "Always oppressed but never conquered."

After the defeat of Germany and her allies, Belgium realized that neutrality on paper gave no protection, that a modern army would be better defense than any treaty against aggression. By the fall of 1939, when World War II began, King Leopold III—his father, King Albert, had been killed in 1934 while mountain climbing in the Ardennes—hoped his people could avoid being drawn into war, even though six hundred thousand Belgians were bearing arms. During the first eight months, while France and Nazi Germany merely bristled at each other from their respective lines of forts, Leopold offered to mediate between them. Then, at dawn on May 10, 1940, without warning, the Nazis attacked neutral Holland, Belgium, and Luxembourg, invading France at the same time. In four days, Holland succumbed to their *blitzkrieg* (lightning war) while French defenses in northern France quickly crumbled. The Belgian Army held for eighteen days of terror, but on May 28, Leopold surrendered.

Though the king and his family were made prisoners first in their palace and then exiled to Switzerland, many Belgian officials and patriots slipped over to England to join British fighting forces. Because the Congo continued to export raw materials vital to the Allies, the government-in-exile established in England could pay its way in the war. Belgian units flying with the Royal Air Force were equipped and maintained by the nation's own funds.

Many who lived through both the first and second German occupations insist the second brought greater hardships, that the enemy was more demanding. For example, the town of Lier, near Antwerp, saw eighty citizens shipped off for labor in Germany. Of these eighty, forty-two eventually came home; the others had died of overwork and undernourishment. Through the bad years, the people again behaved with courage. The rector of Louvain (Leuven) University refused the Nazis a list of his students; he knew they wanted it for the names of young men to ship off to labor camps. He spent eighteen months in prison for this "disobedience."

Just as Ieper recalls British valor in World War I, Bastogne in the Ardennes has become a symbol of American heroism in World War II. The Allied high command reasoned that enemy tanks and motorized equipment could not move easily through the forests that covered this sector of Belgium, so they left it lightly defended. The Nazis surprised them by making a last desperate offensive in force, stabbing here through the woods to surround American units in and around Bastogne. This was mid-December, 1944, a time of icy mists, sleet, and snow. The Allied position looked hopeless, yet when the German commander demanded surrender, the American officer in charge made a short reply: "Nuts," said General Anthony McAuliffe. At last the weather cleared so that Allied air support could come in, while tanks rumbled up as reinforcements. By the last week of January, 1945, the Germans had been defeated—at a cost of 76,890 Allied servicemen killed, lost, or wounded. Most of these casualties were American.

Belgium has not forgotten this Battle of the Bulge. In 1950, funds from a Bastogne postage stamp issued by the Belgian government paid for the sandstone monument which rises from the Hill of Mardasson. From the upper level of this five-pointed, star-shaped open temple you see the town of Bastogne and look out over rolling land. Up high around the walls run the names of the forty-eight states of the U.S. at that time. An account of the Battle of the Bulge is engraved in gold letters around the interior masonry. This severe yet graceful testimony to Belgian gratitude saddens and thrills the visitor.

Except for the penetration into the Ardennes in late 1944, the Nazis had retreated from Belgium by the fall of 1944, leaving too hurriedly to destroy railroads, factories, and dock machinery as they undoubtedly would have done otherwise. No sooner were they gone than the port of Antwerp began handling war supplies; Belgian mills and mines started to produce; parliament met. Since King Leopold was in Switzerland, his brother, Prince Charles, who had fought with the Resistance, acted as regent.

When Leopold III returned from exile he met with hostility from many of his subjects. The Walloons especially resented him for granting unconditional surrender so early in the war. They thought he should have escaped to head his government-in-exile. Because of such intense feeling against him, the people were asked to vote whether or not they wanted him on the throne

The Mardasson Monument honors the Americans who fought in the Battle of the Bulge.

again. Fifty-eight percent favored his remaining as king, but the minority showed opposition by such wholesale violence—strikes and riots—that rather than tear the nation apart he abdicated in favor of his elder son, Baudouin, who became king in 1950 at the age of nineteen.

Baudouin's childhood had been shadowed by personal tragedy. His mother, a Swedish princess whom Belgians loved, had died in an automobile accident when the son was four. His father, at first inconsolable—he had been driving when the accident occurred —later married a rich Flemish woman. Baudouin was nine when the royal family went into exile. Devoted to his father, he resented the animosity toward Leopold on their return. Now that he has matured he is proving to be an able monarch, deeply interested in education, social reforms, and the welfare of his poorer subjects. In 1960 he married a charming and talented Spanish noblewoman, Fabiola de Mora y Aragon. Belgians like her, first because their king seems so much happier now, and also because she keeps out of politics yet is concerned with education and welfare. She goes about with her husband opening new schools, dedicating memorials and bridges, laying wreaths, and visiting hospitals. Baudouin and Fabiola have paid state visits abroad, and Baudouin has made two trips to the Congo—the queen went with him the second time. They live in the suburb of Laeken on a royal estate hidden by spacious wooded grounds. The king's greenhouses, being Belgian, are fabulous. Every morning, Baudouin drives to the town palace in upper Brussels—one knows he is there if his flag flies above the palace.

Their Majesties King Baudouin and Queen Fabiola.

The king and queen have no children, so the heir to the throne is Philippe, the son of Baudouin's brother, Prince Albert. Their sister is married to the Grand Duke of Luxembourg, making a bond between the two countries which is said to be strong. Baudouin speaks French, Flemish, and German, the languages of Belgium, as well as Spanish and fluent English. Those who know him say he has a nice sense of humor. One anecdote illustrates this trait. Some years ago, he stayed for a few days at a golf resort in a southwestern city. The manager, a charming southern woman, welcomed him and said: "You know, I have never talked to a king before, so if you do not mind, I shall not call you Your Majesty, but Mr. King." Baudouin smiled agreement to this. When he returned to Brussels he wrote her a personal letter to thank her for the superb food and good care she had provided. And signed the letter: "Mr. King."

Both World Wars I and II ravaged Belgium; World War II also affected Holland. Intelligent men in both nations realized that, small as these countries were, they could not rely on promises of protection made by powerful neighbors. Even before the end of World War II, they began planning for cooperation, for a solid heartland of Europe. With Belgian statesmen in the lead, they worked out a commercial union of the Netherlands, the Grand Duchy of Luxembourg, and Belgium. The motto of Belgium, "In Union There Is Strength," although not adopted by the coalition, seems to have inspired the formation of Benelux (the acronym formed by combining first syllables of the countries' names). In 1944, Benelux set about abolishing customs duties, immigration restrictions, and other barriers to free trade across frontiers.

The European Economic Community is an outgrowth of this earlier experiment. In 1957, France, Italy, and West Germany united with the Benelux countries to form a larger union with the same goals. This Common Market agreement was signed in Rome. Fifteen years later, in January, 1972, England, Ireland, Norway, and Denmark met with the original six partners in the splendid Egmont Palace of Brussels to sign a second treaty enlarging the European Economic Community. However, in September, 1972, the Norwegians rejected membership in a referendum, so that in January, 1973, the Common Market became a body of nine. Its central office functions in a huge, gray-green building which swings over a vast sunken plaza near downtown Brussels.

The objectives of the group are primarily commercial, but the hope is that gradually, with restrictions to free trade abolished and immigration among the nine member nations unrestricted, well-established political and even cultural interests may bind Europe closer together. In general, Common Market products pass freely from nation to nation. There is no import tax on French perfume in Brussels or Italian shoes in London. Val Saint Lambert crystal must compete with Irish Waterford glass. Each country pays workers according to its own wage scale; no rules govern prices, so goods sell at their homeland price.

Free passage of aliens from one land to another has lately caused some friction. For years, Italian workers came into Belgium to labor in the dangerous coal mines of Wallonia. Now that these veins are exhausted in much of the coal region and mining families struggle to find jobs in new industries being set up in their districts, Belgian workmen, Walloon and Fleming alike, resent competition from the foreigners who have settled among them.

After World War II, two major ideological camps emerged to dominate world politics: the Western powers influenced by the United States, and the Eastern powers inclined to follow Russia's lead. In 1949, twelve Western nations signed the North Atlantic Peace Treaty, creating a defensive alliance. These were Belgium,

Canada, Denmark, France, Iceland, Italy, Luxembourg, Holland, Norway, Portugal, Great Britain, and the United States. Greece and Turkey entered the alliance in 1952, West Germany in 1955. The political arm of the council, called NATO (North Atlantic Treaty Organization), and its European military headquarters (Supreme Allied Command), which is known as SHAPE, are also located in Belgium. (The United States sends three full ambassadors to Belgium. The first is accredited to the government, a second to NATO, and the third to the Common Market, where he acts as a mere observer.)

NATO came to Brussels in 1967 when France declared it un-

Architecturally advanced buildings in Brussels house many international organizations.

welcome there. American and European military and diplomatic experts work at NATO in long concrete buildings that look as though they were just dropped down on an untidy field near the Brussels airport. Original plans had been to build an imposing home in the Brussels suburb of Laeken, where King Baudouin lives, but no member nation felt such expense justified, and these "temporary" headquarters are now considered permanent.

SHAPE, like NATO, is a refugee from France. When the French government asked it to leave, SHAPE went up within five months' time on five hundred acres of flat land near Casteau, a town thirty-five miles below Brussels and only five miles from Mons. Here, too, homes and office buildings are far from impressive. Half the personnel of SHAPE is American; the others represent the Allies with military forces in Western Europe. About twenty-five hundred families live on the base, while another eighteen hundred have houses, villas, or chateaux (depending on their rank) throughout the surrounding countryside.

More than a hundred other international commissions of various types—commercial, electronic, atomic—center in Brussels, which has become the metropolitan capital of the West. Italian, English, Dutch, West German, Canadian, and Turkish military officers, engineers, and economists live and work here. The International School, set in parklike grounds, has an enrollment of fifteen hundred pupils, mainly children of these foreigners, while the DOD (Department of Defense) school accounts for seven hundred more pupils, mostly Americans. Others attend Belgian schools. Businessmen from many nations visit or work in the capital. Now one may say that the "very cockpit of Christendom" has become "the land common to all nations."

8

Antwerp and the North

Belgium today still fascinates the visitor who is not in a hurry to see most of Europe in three or four weeks. Every day means contacts with interesting people, the discovery of unusual places: flower and food markets, churches, museums, old armor and weapons, castles. More than fifty castles stand, most in fine condition. Some still belong to private families; others have been willed to the government or acquired in other fashions. State-owned castles are always open to the public and the others—the private homes—open their parks and handsome interiors to visitors from time to time. In 1971, designated by the General Tourist Bureau as The Year of the Castles, the stranger could cross many a moat, wander through beautifully planted gardens and inspect fine parlors, libraries lined with books, even ancient kitchens. This happened again in 1972. (Not long before, the tourist bureau proclaimed a Year of Museums; once, it even held a Year of the Windmills.) In the summer, too, some castles lend their small theaters or great halls for concerts of chamber music or song recitals to which anyone buying a ticket may go.

Travel by train, bus, and car is easy. Towns lie close together over such good roads that sometimes it is hard to decide which turn to take, what to see; one feels like riding off in all directions at once. In Tournai to the southwest, Ieper is near; so is Ath, just northeast. The giants of Ath are famous, but they appear only on the last weekend in August. Then their dismounted wicker bodies, which have been packed away, are put together and they take over the town: Goliath, huge and ugly, once again marries Madame Victory, just as big and hideous; the following day, he and his bride, attended by numerous other giants, proceed between the crowds through the streets.

Belgium-bound airlines, especially overseas flights, put down at Zaventem, the Brussels airport. A traveler who can take a freighter up the Scheldt to Antwerp enters Belgium in a more dramatic way, for the city rises from land so netted with canals, so caught up in loops of the river that it seems to belong to water. The illusion is more vivid on a rainy day when the single spire of the cathedral, lifting into a low sky from a welter of roofs, looks as though just risen from the water. When Gabriel, the cathedral's big bell, tolls, it might be sounding from a city buried under the sea. Lohengrin, the Knight of the Swan in German legends and poems and the hero of Richard Wagner's opera of the same name, is supposed to have come up river in a skiff drawn by a swan and to have stepped ashore at Antwerp. Such fantasies can last only a moment, though, for all about the port, rated third largest in the world, spread miles of docks where ultramodern equipment loads and unloads ships. Oil storage tanks, motor assembly plants, refineries stretch for acres; buildings which house Belgian and foreign manufacturing works reach everywhere.

Antwerp's commercial history held disasters as well as success. Having inherited the trade which once made Bruges so rich (by mid-fifteenth century, Bruges turned into an inland city because of silting caused by the North Sea), Antwerp prospered. Sea captains, traders, and bankers moved from Bruges to Antwerp, and for a time the town became the busiest port in Europe. Then, after a century of prosperity it, too, died—but not of silt. Antwerp was a war casualty. The tale of its ruin is long and involved, but, briefly, the struggle between Spain and the northern Netherlands for possession of this vital entry from the sea ruined it. The port was blocked during the latter part of the sixteenth century. When peace finally came, Holland held the land on both banks of the Scheldt and refused to reopen the river to the southern Netherlands, thus choking off traffic in or out. Only rarely did a ship move between Antwerp and the North Sea during the next two hundred years. Then in the nineteenth century, while William I ruled a "United Netherlands," the port reopened, only to close again when Belgium broke away from the northern Netherlands. Finally, some time after the treaty of 1839, Holland agreed to allow ship passage.

Despite all the affluence and progress of the present, much of the old Antwerp remains to be seen. Picturesque houses shelter among tall buildings where cars congest the streets and noisy machines gouge out tunnels for a subway system. Wide boulevards seem like disorderly drag strips and present the extra danger of cars that plunge out from almost any narrow street to the right. At a corner here and there in a busy neighborhood an ancient statue of the Blessed Virgin smiles down from her niche above a doorway. Here stands a massive gateway, once part of the town fortifications. The tall, turreted House of the Butchers is downtown. Vehicles rattle over cobbled streets en route to a center city office building or bank.

Guild houses frame the vast cobbled Grote Markt, where the heroic figure of Brabo, the legendary slayer of the tyrannical giant Antigoon, poises over the body of the dead monster. This group makes a fountain without a basin; water jets out and down over the cobbles, trickling off in every direction. The guild houses look as splendid as those in Brussels, yet they seem less spectacular because they lack gilded faces. Handsome rooms in the town hall on this square are wood-paneled, tapestry-hung, decorated with murals. One displays the bronze tablet General Eisenhower presented when he was supreme Allied commander. This plaque commends the citizens of the town for their heroism during seven months of German rocket bomb attacks. After the Allies had recovered the port—that is, from mid-October, 1944, until the last of May, 1945—rockets killed three thousand men, women, and children and destroyed twenty thousand buildings. Yet Antwerp never halted the business of keeping Allied shipping on the move.

A bomb exploding in the Friday Market before the Plantin Museum shattered windows, cracked walls, and ripped open the roof. The contents of the house had been packed away beforehand, and so careful repairs after the war restored this page of history. The structure held the home and shop of the Plantin-Moretus family, whose presses turned out the finest books in the Netherlands.

Christopher Plantin, a Frenchman, founded the business, buying the house here at the corner of Holy Ghost Street and the Market in 1579; he called it the Golden Compass. Later, he added adjoining buildings to the first one. With the help of scholars from Leuven and other universities in Europe, Plantin undertook to publish the Polyglot Bible, so called because on its pages Latin, Greek, Hebrew, Syrian, and Chaldean texts appear in parallel columns. The project delighted King Philip II but almost beggared Plantin because Philip was too miserly to pay him for the cost of the work.

After Plantin's death, his son-in-law, Jan Moretus, maintained the same standards of learning and craftsmanship. Later descendants gradually lost the firm's reputation for excellence. However, out of respect for tradition they preserved every possible shred of

The building that housed a printing firm from the sixteenth century is now the Plantin-Moretus Museum.

the past with such care that when in 1876, a Moretus closed the business and sold the house to the city of Antwerp so it could be opened as a museum of printing—the only one in the world—as well as an example of the typical home of a rich and cultured family.

Everything in the stone and brick mansion is so complete, so authentic that the owner and his staff might have just left it for a moment to watch a parade going down the street. Presses, cases of type, foundries with molds, anvils, grindstones, and the melting furnace wait for leisurely inspection. The small dark shop with barred windows opens on Holy Ghost Street. On its long counter stand scales once used by merchants to weigh coins paid them so they could be sure of the gold and silver content. Portraits of the Plantin and Moretus family, eighteen of which Peter Paul Rubens painted, line the walls. Walls of other rooms are hung with tapestry or covered by leather embossed in intricate designs and gilded.

One case of rare books published by the firm contains a colored sketch said to be the first ever made of the potato plant and the potato after it came from the New World. In the courtyard, where moss turns the cobbles green, a vine clinging to the walls is said to have been planted by Christopher Plantin himself.

Peter Paul Rubens, a friend of Balthazar Moretus, Plantin's grandson, painted the Plantin-Moretus family and also made etchings to illustrate books put out by the firm. Rubens is the outstanding figure of a group of Flemish artists, as famous as those other masters of earlier centuries, men like Jan and Hubert van Eyck, Hans Memling, and Rogier van der Weyden, among others. He inspired his fellow painters of the seventeenth century and might be said to have founded a school of painting, yet he emerges most clearly not by comparison with his followers but by contrast with a painter who died eight years before he was born. This man was Peter Brueghel. Both Brueghel and Rubens are Flemish to the bone, but each saw the world in his own fashion. In spite of a lifetime spent in Brussels, Brueghel remained a peasant at heart. Rubens, court painter for Archduchess Isabella and a friend of kings, nobles, and scholars, was something of a scholar himself. He served on top diplomatic missions. Brueghel depicted the life of peasants and plain people; Rubens painted portraits of aristocrats and enormous church canvases and allegorical scenes to please royal critics. Brueghel is humorous, wry, cynical; Rubens, urbane, lavish, charmed with the society he knows. Each man represents the era and class to which he belonged.

Brueghel is more the historian than Rubens. Scenes he recorded with his brush give as full an account of his friends as if he had used pen and paper to write about them. He brings to life guests at a country wedding feast, harvesters resting in a field of yellow wheat, peasants dancing, children stealing birds' nests. To this day, the Brabant landscape waits for him to paint again with his precise outlines its feathery trees and swelling fields of grain.

Brueghel's *The Census at Bethlehem* sets a biblical incident in a busy, earthy Flemish landscape.

The woman delivering milk, a taxicab driver, the fat man dozing on a park bench—all might be just about to pose for him.

Brueghel's genius is individual; no other artist was so humorous and yet clear-eyed. Rubens, too, has a style particularly his own, even though he taught young painters, many of whom were influenced by his genius. He painted in the grand manner, with freedom, strength, and a mastery of color that delighted his own age and still impress artists and critics. The great of Europe sat for him. When Isabella sent him to Spain on a diplomatic mission, the king and his grandees commissioned forty portraits. The queen of France ordered twenty-one gigantic pictures to mark the chief events of her life. Two of his finest portraits, hanging in the Museum of Ancient Art in Brussels, are of Albert and Isabella. Albert is shown in profile, a thin, severe man. Isabella, plump and elderly, dressed in black with a white ruff and ropes of pearls, looks tired and worried, yet amiable.

Rubens' masterpiece is not a portrait, but rather *The Descent from the Cross,* a religious painting in the Cathedral of Antwerp which shows the apostles taking the body of the dead Christ from the cross. Art critics speak of the body of Christ as the finest human figure ever painted. The grouping of the other figures is superb, while tenderness and grief on every face emphasize a human rather than a divine tragedy.

Rubens possessed untiring energy. When not abroad on some mission for the archduchess, he spent his days at home working at top speed—making designs for illustrations for Plantin-Moretus books, remodeling his house in Antwerp, listening to someone read aloud from a scholarly book, criticizing the canvases of his pupils. His house in Antwerp does not bring him to life so startlingly as the Plantin Museum evokes its occupants, perhaps because the former is a reconstruction, a skillful reproduction but not the original. Nevertheless, the place has charm, especially the

Courtyard in Rubens's house.

garden, of which he has given a glimpse in a painting of himself and his second wife, Helene Fourment. A noisy, crowded street detracts from the façade of the house, but the garden stretches green and quiet past flower beds to a long green arbor.

Indoors, as seen from a balcony, the two-story studio seems peopled with students working at their easels while he walks among them, suggesting, retouching, perhaps praising. A door to the right of the balcony reaches up to the ceiling, built so high in order to let enormous paintings be moved out easily when finished. Since no painting left his studio until he had corrected and retouched it, since he first planned and sketched out the work as he wanted it to be, each canvas is in a sense his; all reflect his love of lavish outlines and luscious color. His preliminary sketches or small paintings that served the students as guides are exquisite.

While Anthony van Dyck studied under Rubens, he used to

paint the most difficult parts of these cooperative works, because the master recognized the young man's rare talent. In a short life, van Dyck became a fashionable portrait painter. He did not bring out in his subjects the reality and individuality of Rubens' sitters, but he made them look aristocratic and as handsome as they imagined they were. Most of his works hang in England, where he spent the last years of his life, but Brussels and Antwerp own a few. Numerous museums in the United States also have good van Dycks, as well as paintings by Rubens and a few works of fifteenth-century masters like the two van Eycks and sixteenth-century Memling.

On a pleasant day in Antwerp, the waterfront near the Steen offers a fine observation post. The small boats which nose down the Scheldt past grinding cranes and winches, past ships tied up at wharves, take on and discharge passengers near the Steen. This ancient, turreted fortress became in time a prison; now, crumbling, it houses a collection of ship models and other maritime exhibits. Tourists may rest on a bench in the shade of trees lining the bank where it stands. Or they may enjoy a walk over its drawbridge through a cobbled courtyard to the terrace overlooking the river, where seagulls swoop low and the masts of some freighter, perhaps from Greece or the United States, reach as high as the terrace railing.

Antwerp citizens tell you they prosper so long as the port functions. Their other great industry, until oil refineries and other foreign enterprises came not long ago, has been diamond cutting. Thousands of craftsmen cut and polish gray, soapy pebbles into brilliant stones. Craftsmen have worked at this since the sixteenth century. However, during World War II, most of them escaped to other countries, because so many diamond cutters were Jews. Many of those remaining waited out the war in Nazi concentration camps.

The Antwerp zoo near the main railroad station downtown deserves a visit. City parks, like all Belgian parks, are gay and green
in spring and summer. Antwerp has fine museums. At night, life
on the main streets suggest a *paseo* in some Spanish or Latin-
American city. Everyone comes out to walk the neon-lighted
streets, where trees throw weird shadows on the brightness. Sailors,
just home from Africa, Brazil, or the Near East swagger through
the crowds; here is an Arab, probably off some freighter. Well-
dressed, good-looking citizens stream along, chattering, laughing,
stopping to talk to friends, drifting in and out of cafes, lining up
before a movie theater where a popular film, perhaps American,
may be showing. Antwerp is hard to leave.

9

Lier, Mechelen, and Leuven

Departure from Antwerp brings up again the nagging question: which way? Southwest through farmlands where North Sea winds beat at the remaining windmills and blow ocean spray? Fifteen miles in that direction lies Sint-Niklaas (Saint Nicholas) with the largest public square in Belgium. That is not why Sint-Niklaas deserves a visit. Even its fine ancient buildings are not so interesting as two large rooms in the museum which are dedicated to Gerhardus Mercator, the sixteenth-century geographer, who was born nearby. Meridians on the Mercator map of the world are drawn parallel, thus making North America look larger than South America. The exhibit in Sint-Niklaas contains maps he drew, copies of books he wrote, and two globes he made, one of crystal showing the heavens and the other of wood, representing the earth.

Instead of going to Sint-Niklaas, one may prefer to return to Brussels by way of Lier, called by many the prettiest town in Belgium, and certainly in Flanders. Its spires and treetops are outlined against the pale sky. A belfry with a turret flanks the town hall. The thin River Nethe coils through shaded banks in town, then out into the fields. Gabled houses look through shining windows at clean, narrow streets. A unique road sign, said to be the only medieval example of its kind, surmounts a tall iron standard. The sign itself consists of two markers cut out of iron and brightly painted, which are attached almost at a right angle. Each is a miniature stagecoach ending in a hand with a finger pointing to a nearby village. Of late, Ghent has put up the same kind of signs in town, but they lack the charm of this ancient one.

In the béguinage, behind the high wall protecting it from the streets, flags flap against red and white brick housefronts. Some are Belgian; others, flags of the Flemish provinces. If it is First Communion Sunday, women work outside, scrubbing doorsills and sprinkling the streets with confetti. After the service in the béguinage church, the children who have just made their first solemn Communion will march down the flag-hung way between the houses, over cobbles and confetti, carrying banners and singing.

Poor families live in the Lier béguinage now, because all the women of the order have gone. Beguines were groups of women found only in Belgium, with the exception of several groups in Holland. The eight-hundred-year-old order resembles many sisterhoods of nuns except that, unlike a nun, a Beguine did not take permanent religious vows; she could at any time go back to life in the world. In the Middle Ages rich and noble women often entered a béguinage for a life of prayer and piety, bringing fortunes with them. Such prosperity ended long ago and béguinages have been poor for generations. Many no longer exist; only a few elderly Beguines live on in such establishments as the Small Béguinage of Ghent. Most of these women earn a living by fine sewing, lace-making, going out to nurse. One rarely sees a Beguine any more in the traditional habit of full black gown and wide white Flemish headdress.

Buyers for American stores know Lier for beaded bags, lace, and brass musical instruments made there. Visitors think of it as

The béguinage at Bruges.

the location of the Zimmer Tower, a cream-colored seventeenth-century structure which, in 1930, was renamed for Louis Zimmer, a local watchmaker and astronomer. In that year, Zimmer installed in the tower a system of dials controlled by a clock mechanism. The clock, with twelve other dials encircling it, covers the upper third of one face of the tower. The dials give a variety of information: one indicates the day of the month, another the day of the week, a third lets you compute the weekday on which every date falls within a cycle of twenty-eight years. The prettiest dial shows phases of the moon. A globe in low relief turns its blue-painted side at the dark of the moon; as the moon waxes, it grows from a golden sliver to a full gold face, then dwindles again with the waning.

A second-floor room of the tower contains fifty-seven dials covering the walls with information as to the hour here and there in the world. What time is it in Turkey, the Philippines, the west

Inside the Zimmer Tower, fifty-seven more dials also show the time.

coast of the United States? What about high or low tides off Iceland, the coast of Viet Nam, or Portugal? The planets revolve about the sun. One dial marks the hour according to a decimal system which divides night and day into ten hours altogether, each hour being 140 minutes long. This type of clock was used only in the French Revolution. The guide who points it out predicts that, while decimal time was the time of the past, it will one day be the time of the future.

Malines, only a few miles south of Lier, was long the city associated with music, lace, and white asparagus. Now Malines appears on the map as Mechelen, which is its Flemish name. All other cities in Flanders are likewise designated by Flemish rather than French names now.

Farms surround Mechelen. Trucks haul big sweet strawberries and other produce to nearby Brussels. Not long ago, farmers sent their fruit and vegetables by wagon or barge. Now quays along the River Dyle lie empty except for an occasional barge bringing in other merchandise. In winter and spring, fishing boats put in with loads of mussels. The Dyle still smells brackish; North Sea winds still scour houses that front on the river and tides come up just as when Mechelen was a bustling port.

Four hundred years ago, when Margaret of Austria acted as regent for her nephew Charles V, she made Mechelen the capital of the Netherlands. Margaret, the daughter of Emperor Maximilian and Mary of Burgundy, had inherited true Burgundian love of art and learning. Musicians and scholars, artists and architects came to her court; she kept the latter busy carving, chiseling, painting, and building. The palace where she brought up young Charles and his sisters after the death of their father and the onset of their mother's insanity is now the courthouse, a building with a steep slate roof studded by small gabled windows overlooking a grassy courtyard.

Saint Rombaut's Cathedral, begun in the thirteenth century, long before Margaret's time, looms above gables and high-walled gardens. It was badly damaged by fire in August, 1972, but many paintings and art objects were saved and Belgium will certainly restore this architectural treasure. In the summer, visitors have often gone out from Brussels to hear concerts played on its carillon, which has been called "the sweetest voice in Belgium."

In early Netherlands history, bells warned of storm, fire, and invaders, but their voices did not blend into music. In the fourteenth century, mechanical clocks installed in church towers and town belfries could move the bells to make them toll the hour, the half and quarter hours. When the bells could be controlled mechanically, more and more were added until their range of tones fused into tunes, usually played just before the clock struck. Thus, the carillon became a musical instrument. Later, addition of a keyboard enabled a musician to play the carillon somewhat as he would a pipe organ, with small bells moved by hand and heavy ones by foot pedals.

About fifty years ago, Jef Denyn, carillonneur of Saint Rombaut's, founded in Mechelen the only school of carillon music in the world. He taught musicians who went back to fine bell towers in the United States and other countries; new generations have studied under his successors. In 1953 the school dedicated its own carillon, located in a slim red-brick tower flanked by red-brick buildings and surrounded by green lawns which are hidden behind a high wall. The whole edifice looks as though it belongs to the background of a Flemish painting.

If one climbs up to see its carillon, he looks over row after row of bells, hung tier above tier, the largest fitted into heavy framework below the lighter ones, which swing from upper frames in order of diminishing size and weight. The biggest bells are taller than a man and weigh as much as eight tons; the smallest are ten to twelve inches high and a mere twenty pounds light.

Belgium once had more than a hundred singing towers; today about sixty remain. Cities like Mechelen, Ghent, and Bruges schedule regular keyboard concerts on summer evenings; for other occasions the bells play mechanical music turned out by perforated cylinders which look like the disks of a giant old music box, revolving as they play. Pins set in the perforations form a musical pattern for each song, hymn, or patriotic air which peals out.

Once a city of lacemakers, Mechelen has almost lost the art. Now one rarely if ever sees a woman sitting outside her door on a fine day with a pillow before her, weaving threads from countless bobbins through a maze of pins that prick out the design of a pattern stretched over the pillow. In the old days, the spectator might have watched those twisting threads fill birds, butterflies, flowers, and figures into a delicate mesh. Shops in many cities still sell handmade lace, although the shop owners say that very little of it is bobbin lace, but rather a type made with needle and thread. Lace-making has been taught in Belgium for generations, usually in convents, where women work together, singing old ballads about biblical characters, saints, or heroes of legend, as well as some popular songs. The music always carries a strong rhythm to which their hands work in time. Types of Belgian lace vary; lace is different in Lier, Bruges, Binche, and Brussels. Bobbin lace from Brussels is always chosen for a court train or a wedding veil; a veil can cost as much as three thousand dollars.

A good way to see Belgium is to settle down in Brussels and go out for one-day excursions. Parts of the country are fascinating, that is, if one can tolerate ugly factory districts and not look too hard at files of new brick, boxlike houses marching down many a road, especially in Flanders. Each house boasts a large picture window, shining, usually without curtains, and defended by rows of stiff plants in copper pots set across the windowsill. One comes to loathe this particular kind of plant.

The trip from Brussels to Leuven (Louvain) is short; yet here the land swells gently as though lifting towards the Ardennes. The outskirts of town have tree-shaded esplanades, but center streets are narrow and crowded and busy. The town hall stands

amid this huddle of buildings and that seems too bad, because
Leuven's town hall is one of the truly beautiful buildings of Europe. It should be carved ivory instead of stone and shrunk to
jewel-case size, so delicate and elaborate is its architecture. Mirac-
ulously, both World Wars spared it, as well as the white and yellow houses of the equally ancient béguinage. War landmarks in
Leuven have been restored according to old plans, so that it often
recalls a town of the Middle Ages; turrets, spires, gables, and cobbled streets follow the meanders of the River Dyle.

Women of Leuven, in regional costume for a local pageant, pass by the
elaborate town hall.

Since 1425 the Catholic University of Louvain (as it was always called until recently) ranked as one of the most famous universities in Europe. It remains the outstanding school in the nation, offering instruction in every major field, including theology. Today some twenty-five thousand students, including three thousand foreigners, attend classes there. Illustrious men have studied here: a fifteenth-century pope; Charles V, for a short time; Erasmus, the Dutch humanist and scholar, who influenced Protestantism without ever leaving the Catholic fold. Mercator, the geographer, studied at Louvain, as did Sir (Saint) Thomas More of England. The first edition of More's book about an ideal society, his *Utopia,* came off the Louvain University press.

Americans feel almost at home when visiting the university library, for it stands as a symbol of Belgian-American friendship. After World War I, people in the United States contributed most of the money needed to construct a new library to replace the one burned by the Germans. An American architect designed the present building with its steep Flemish roof and marble façade lighted by long leaded windows. In the deep, covered entrance porch, every pillar bears, carved in gold letters, the name of some group that contributed to the reconstruction fund: Parochial Schools of New York City, Johns Hopkins University, the University of Texas, Friends Central School of Philadelphia, and many others.

World War II bombing again burned the books but did not destroy the library building beyond repair. Nor did it ruin the tower rising from an inner court. Here hang fifty-eight bells of a carillon presented by the engineers of the United States. The Germans took down bells from many other towers and shipped them away, but this carillon escaped such a fate; the giant bell still hangs in the tower. It bears this inscription: "The Liberty Bell of Louvain. The Carillon in Memory of the Engineers of the

United States of America, who gave their Lives in the service of their country and her Allies in the Great War of 1914–1918." Looking up at the tower, one notices a clock dial which shows twelve stars instead of numerals to mark the hours. Each of the other three sides bears a similar dial, thus making forty-eight stars in all, one for each state of the union at the time of that war.

Now the university has changed. A six-hundred-year-old tradition was shattered when Flemish-Walloon differences split the institution into two camps: the Catholic University of Leuven (the original school), and the new Catholic University, known as Louvain-la-Neuve. Language caused the rift. For years, some classes had been held in Flemish, others in French. Two separate universities functioned in the one city. The Flemings resented such an arrangement, claiming that Leuven stood on Flemish soil (ten miles north of the linguistic frontier in Flemish Brabant) and that the city had grown too small to accommodate such a large student body. Therefore they demanded that the French section of the university move elsewhere. Their anger vented itself in rioting. In January, 1968, many marched through the streets, protesting wildly. Some Flemings even broke into offices of French professors and burned books and manuscripts found there. Everywhere appeared slogans such as "Walloons, go home," or "Flanders for the Flemish."

The demonstrations rocked Belgium. In the capital hot debate erupted in parliament, in streets, in newspapers. The Belgian cabinet fell because of the dispute. When a new government took office, it decreed that as soon as possible classes in the university of the old city should go on in Flemish only, while a French campus should be established south of the linguistic border at a site to be called Louvain-la-Neuve.

School by school, Louvain-la-Neuve has opened, about thirty-five minutes by train from downtown Brussels. It occupies a wooden plateau made interesting by a little river and four valleys. Architects plan a quiet academic retreat among lovely Belgian woods; no car may enter the heart of the small town about which school buildings are located. Removal from Leuven progresses with the work of building, with third- and fourth-year physics and mathematics classes meeting in the new school in 1972, and the faculties of architecture and chemistry going out in 1973. By 1977, the entire French university will function at Louvain-la-Neuve.

10

Rich Ghent

On Christmas Eve, 1814, a group of men gathered in a mansion of Ghent to sign the treaty which ended the War of 1812 between the United States and England. The chief American delegate was John Quincy Adams, who, eleven years later, became the sixth president of the United States. When the ceremony ended, Ghent's belfry rang out news of Christmas peace. Today, the house, now the Museum of the Treaty of Ghent, displays a copy of that treaty, while portraits of the signers and a painting of the peace ceremony hang on the walls of the room where the meeting took place. The house itself, once the home of an aristocrat of Ghent, is a museum of French furniture, jade ornaments, and Chinese porcelains.

As to the belfry, an eleven-foot-high dragon lords over its summit. Some citizens claim the creature came from Constantinople; others believe it as Flemish as the stout tower. No one mentions the fact that Dragon the First, which went up in 1377, abdicated a hundred years ago to a shining new copy of itself. If you take the elevator which limps up through the tower, you may get off at the floor where the original dragon, worn to a black metal skeleton by the winds of East Flanders, reposes with other mementos such as ancient bells, models of the belfry at various stages of its history, even one of Napoleon's big hats. Framework on another level supports the big bells. On a third story are the metal disks pricked out with tunes to be played mechanically. A keyboard nearby is played by the carillonneur to use for special concerts, such a small keyboard to move all fifty-two bells, large and small.

Ghent of the splendid and tempestuous past has stood for more than a thousand years where the Rivers Lieve and Leie join the Scheldt. It is a water city on a mass of eighty, some say one hundred, islands, linked together by two hundred bridges, yet it prefers to be called "the city of flowers." As suitable a name might be "the city of contrasts." Gray stone and dark brick frown down on blooming gardens around them, old buildings huddle among new ones, the citizens combine keen business interest and industry with a gift of elegance and a love of beauty. No community has a larger number of haughty aristocrats, yet nowhere in the country is socialism stronger.

The statue to the weavers of Ghent is a landmark. Ancient patrician houses stand as showpieces, many still owned by local families. Ghent, the art city, is also a key industrial center. Men grow rich here from linen and cotton mills as well as in the newer petrochemical works, in steel making, in shipping. Ultramodern apartments have replaced some old houses, but the Graslei (Quay of Herbs) still stretches its quaint high houses along the canal where once hay and grain were brought by barges to the wharf. The Graslei stands very still these days. No traffic stirs the waters of the canal at its foot, because all barges have been diverted to the new port.

Several fortresses remain, but the one built after the Battle of Waterloo has been razed to make way for Citadel Park, a reach of lawns and ponds. In May the air here is fragrant with lilacs, shaded by red-flowering hawthorn trees. Spring and summer through, beds of tulips, pansies, begonias, roses bloom. The Floralia Palace, standing in the park, welcomes a million or more visitors every fifth year (1970, 1975, and so on through the future) to one of the world's great flower shows, the Floralies. In intervening years other flower shows occupy the building: a pageant in September, a mid-September horticultural society exhibit every other year. The University of Ghent School of Botany and Horticulture cares for the local botanical gardens, an enchanting place of greenhouses with an indoor orange garden.

In the center of town, near the belfry, stands Sint Baafs Cathedral, begun when Ghent was young. From the exterior it looks heavy and forbidding; inside, it is a clutter of black and white

The Floralies, Ghent's international flower show.

marble, paintings, carved wood, gold and silver vessels, gleaming bronze. A rear chapel displays the panels of *The Adoration of the Mystic Lamb* by the brothers van Eyck.

The Sint Jorishof has stood near the belfry for six hundred years. Still an excellent hotel, it belongs to the history of Flanders. The lion carved into the vast mantelpiece of one of its dining rooms commemorates the fact that in this great hall Mary of Burgundy signed a charter of liberty for Flanders. For more than five centuries, the Sint Jorishof has been headquarters for the Guild of Sint Joris (Saint George), the order of crossbowmen. When the crossbow became merely a piece of sports equipment, not a weapon, many Belgians still practiced shooting. A former owner of the Sint Jorishof was crossbow champion of Europe.

Reflected in the waters of the Lieve, the Castle of the Counts of Flanders shows what a Crusader's castle in the Holy Land must have looked like, for it is modeled after such a fortress. Sentries probably peered through slits in its battlements at bloody fights between citizens and members of warring local guilds. In the Hundred Years' War, King Edward III of England banqueted in the castle with his ally, Jacob van Artevelde. In one hall, while fiddlers played, Duke Philip of Burgundy feasted with his Knights of the Golden Fleece. Charles V, who was born in Ghent, frequently came to the castle. Ghosts of prisoners taken in struggles between towns, between guilds, between town and ruler, must haunt the dungeons and torture chambers.

Two smaller fortresses also remain. Arcades of rounded arches in the underground vaults of the Castle of Gerard the Devil give a perfect example of medieval architecture. The second fortress, the Rabot, spans the River Lieve; it consists of two strong, squat towers, one on each side of the stream. When Charles punished Ghent for its revolt against him, he destroyed city walls and fortifications, but did not touch the Rabot, which also formed part of

Aerial view of the Castle of the Counts of Flanders.

the defenses. Although Charles as a young man had been popular in Ghent, the citizens came to detest him. They made no effort to preserve the splendid palace where he was born. Now, all that marks the site in an old neighborhood is an arch and a crumbling fragment of wall surmounted by several small turrets.

By way of contrast to its warlike spirit, Ghent has always been devout. Church towers punctuate the skyline and it has not one but two béguinages, the Old Béguinage, now abandoned, and the Small Béguinage. Thirty to forty elderly women live on in the Small Béguinage, each in her tiny red-brick, stone-trimmed house, which bears a polished brass nameplate: Huis (House) of Our Lady of Lourdes, House of Saint Modestus, House of Saint Eleanor, of Mary Magdalen. The Beguines wear the traditional costume of their order and worship in their church on the béguinage square.

Long ago Ghent erected a statue to Jacob van Artevelde; only recently, one to Charles V. These two men, one admired and the other disliked, typify the strong, violent city. The third famous son is associated with France rather than Belgium. He is Maurice Maeterlinck, a Nobel-prize-winning poet and dramatist of our own century, who died in 1949. Though born and educated in Ghent (in French), Maeterlinck left his birthplace as a young man to live in France. Not until he became famous did the town regret its mockery of his early writings. He never returned except on family matters.

Maeterlinck's dreamy, whimsical plays are in French, yet he remains as Flemish as Flanders. Photographs show full lips, a broad face, an air of quiet strength. His precise stage directions for every play recall the painstaking details of a Flemish painting. His *Blue Bird,* which gave his generation a symbol for happiness, his *Pelléas and Mélisande,* the haunting tragedy that so charmed the composer Claude Debussy that he used it as the libretto for an opera, reveal an imagination as Flemish as a dragon weathervane, as fanciful as the giants or great cat figures, as flaunting as the knights in armor and ladies in silks who parade the streets of Belgian towns at festival time.

If Maeterlinck were a young man in Ghent today, his education might have been Flemish rather than French, for in Flanders all elementary and secondary schools, as well as the University of Ghent, now teach in Netherlandish. Belgium offers a choice of four universities: Ghent and Leuven are wholly Dutch; the Free

University of Brussels is divided into two sections, one Flemish, the other French; Liège, the most French of any Belgian city, has a French university, while Louvain-la-Neuve, when completed, will be French also. In 1965, two other cities were given incomplete universities, called university centers. A student at Antwerp can study science, economics, medicine, or language translation and interpretation. The Prince Leopold School of Tropical Medicine enjoys renown at home and abroad. Mons (French) teaches physics, chemistry, applied sciences, education and another series of classes in translating and interpreting foreign languages.

Belgian education has changed over the last twenty-five to thirty years. When the nation declared its independence from Holland, even Flemish students complained if the teaching was in Netherlandish, not French. Accordingly, Ghent became a French university, a change from the Dutch which King William had stipulated when he founded the institution. However, with the growth of Flamingant feeling, demands rose for a Dutch school. Nothing was done about this until World War I, when the Germans, anxious to woo the Flemish and divide Belgian loyalties, reinstated Dutch. A few ardent Flamingants approved the move, but many others resented outside interference. Some even wrote the German authorities to say, in effect, "We are a people which has always managed its own affairs on its own soil." The innovation lasted one year. With the German retreat, Ghent became French again; not until 1930 did the government convert it to Flemish. In 1955, King Baudouin, with other prominent Belgians, attended ceremonies marking the school's twenty-fifth anniversary as Flemish.

11

Bruges Is Not Dead

Some poet once wrote of "Bruges the Dead," coining a phrase which should have been worn out long ago from overuse. Almost every tourist who reads a guidebook knows the expression; the words cast a melancholy spell and at first seem appropriate. However, they do not describe the spirit of the ancient city nor its present outlook. Bruges may seem to dream, but it is not dead, merely breathing slowly.

If Bruges appears untouched by time, this is a carefully preserved look. Intelligent city officials see that the nearness of the growing port of Zeebrugge does not disturb the picturesque center of town, guarding every vestige of the past. Yet Bruges the Dead is the site of one of the most progressive schools in Europe, the College of Europe. This small institution, opened in 1950, looks to the future, considering the problems of Europe in relation to the rest of the world. Each year, from early October until the end of May, some sixty graduate students, men and women, all under thirty years old, live at the school, associating with experts in law, political science, economic history, geography, who have come to lecture there. Students not only attend lectures, they also have time to discuss with these scholars such matters of interest as European economic relations with Japan, or Swiss neu-

The drowsy medieval atmosphere of Bruges is carefully preserved.

trality, or the North Atlantic Treaty Organization (NATO) and its role in continental life. Applicants are not limited to Belgians and Europeans. Between 1950 and 1960, about seventy North Americans spent a season of study at the school. One curious aspect of the establishment is that, in spite of the Flemish-Walloon dispute, the two languages required of a student in Flemish Bruges are French and English.

Bruges keeps its narrow cobbled streets; swans drift down canals; trees sketch patterns on dark walls beside the water. Miniature gables cap tiny, cream-colored houses built centuries ago to shelter the city's poor. An order of nuns occupies the ivory and rose-red houses around the square in the béguinage. The nuns make lace and embroidery to sell and, for a few Belgian francs, lead tours through the home of a Beguine as it must have looked long ago—four small rooms enclosing a tiny courtyard and furnished with porcelain stove, heavy furniture, and blue earthenware dishes.

Although not large, Bruges is a tiring place, because as one walks about, something always tempts one around another corner: a crumbling coat of arms over a doorway, a saint's statue in a niche, a weathervane, a balcony swung out over the water, a garden seen through the gate in a high wall. Each quay, every bridge over a canal spans a vista of turrets, towers and gardens, a view of gables in rickrack or scallops against the skyline.

The belfry dominates the town. Simple, yet graceful, it rises from the cloth hall where, in the days of Bruges's greatness, wool merchants bargained and feasted with traders from England and Russia or bankers from Italy. The tower dwarfs the cloth hall; it may loom too large over the square, yet it is splendid, thrusting up from foundations laid on thousands of stakes driven into the marshy ground.

The Chapel of Saint Basil in the shadow of the belfry really comprises two chapels, a dark, low-vaulted crypt and a sanctuary above, gilded and painted. People usually call Saint Basil's the Chapel of the Holy Blood because the upper part was built to hold the golden casket said to contain drops of blood which Christ shed while on the cross. Thierry of Alsace, Count of Flanders, brought the relic home from the Second Crusade and gave it to the city. Citizens consider it their most precious treasure. Every year, on the first Sunday after May second, the golden vessel holding the relic is carried with ancient pageantry to the cathedral, where high mass is said; then it is returned to Saint Basil's. Clergy, church societies, aristocrats of Bruges, citizens wearing armor or costumes copied from the Middle Ages form the procession that accompanies the Holy Blood. On some years, a religious play performed on a high platform in the market square completes the celebration.

Masterpieces of Hans Memling hang in the Hospital of Saint John, not too far from Saint Basil's, and a small chapel of the hospital contains the tombs of Mary of Burgundy and her father, Charles the Bold. They lie asleep in gilded brass effigy side by side. Charles wears armor with helmet and gauntlets beside him; his feet rest on a crouching lion. Mary's two little dogs sleep at her feet, and her many coats of arms in brilliant enamels cover the sides of the tomb. She looks young and royal in an embroidered mantle and tight cap beneath her crown, which is set back from a very high forehead; her hands are folded in prayer. She might be a figure Memling has painted in blue and rose and cream.

Bruges keeps its medieval buildings in fine repair. The city looks spotless, flowers bloom on the quays and in baskets hung from lamp posts, the carillon of the belfry spatters musical notes before the clock strikes. At night, the landmarks are floodlighted.

The past lives, too, in a dark red, fifteenth-century palace on the outskirts of town. This house belongs to the Guild of Saint Sebastian, the longbowmen. Formerly a powerful corporation, the guild has become a club in Bruges. Its members claim the guild existed when longbowmen went from Bruges and other cities of the Netherlands to the First Crusade. Some historians, however, say the archers with the longbow did not organize until two hundred years later, just after the Battle of the Golden Spurs. Of course, this type of bow was in use long before then. The question of dates seems important because members of the rival Guild of Saint George insist their order of crossbowmen was established

Sarcophagi of Mary of Burgundy and Charles the Bold.

nearly a hundred years before the Battle of the Golden Spurs.

Both groups were powerful in the Middle Ages; a corps of skilled bowmen might decide a battle. Rulers sought help from the hardy, independent archers of the Netherlands. In Ghent, Brussels, and cities other than Bruges, counts and dukes competed with weavers, gardeners, brewers, and bankers for championship, either with crossbow or longbow. Even a king coveted the title of *Schutterskoning, Roi du Tir* (King of the Range). In Brussels, Charles V, who loved sports, shot down a wooden bird set up as a target on the spire of Our Lady of Victories, the church near the Square of the Petit Sablon (Square of the Little Sandhill). This feat made him king of archers.

When gunpowder outdated bows and arrows, the Belgians, as

always loyal to tradition, changed archery from a war skill to a sport. In Bruges, archers of Saint Sebastian shoot with sharp-tipped aluminum arrows at a target set far down a long alley of clipped trees, or else go out into a meadow beyond the alley hedge to shoot wooden arrows from the protection of a roofed-over stand at wooden birds swinging from a hundred-foot-high pole. The boys who retrieve arrows and birds wear heavy hats of braided willow with brims wide enough to protect their shoulders from falling objects. An ash tree planted in the right spot shades the archers' eyes during late afternoon hours, the time when a competition invariably begins.

The best shot becomes a king of the guild. In Bruges he keeps the honor for life, whereas some archery clubs make the champion defend his title every year. On great occasions a king wears about his neck a silver-gilt chain from which dangles a silver-gilt falcon; he carries a scepter topped by another gleaming bird. In the long hall of the palace, portraits of guild kings and presidents (head men) line one wall. Beneath them stand ancient cannon no higher than a man's knee. These are wheeled out and fired on the club anniversary in June and again on Saint Sebastian's day in January.

At one end of the room shelves hold silver cups given by famous members, some of whom are honorary, like Queen Victoria of England. She presented two cups, the first in 1843 when she was invited to join, the second in 1893 to mark her fiftieth year of membership. Queen Elizabeth II of England and her husband, Prince Philip, also belong on an honorary basis. Elizabeth sent a handsome cup and she and Philip posed for special photographs which they signed and gave the club.

One English king enjoyed active membership during two years of exile in the Netherlands. While Charles II lived in Bruges between 1656 and 1658, under sentence of death if he returned to an England ruled by Oliver Cromwell, he passed many hours practicing in the meadow and the alley of the dark red palace. A spy for Cromwell reported: "He passes his time with shooting at Bruges and such other obscure pastimes." After Cromwell's death Charles went home and sent a large sum of money for repairs and improvements to the guild house. His marble bust occupies a place of honor on the wall above the fireplace.

The commercial greatness of Bruges ended with the silting of the River Zwyn; then the towns of Damme and Sluis on the Zwyn, nearer the North Sea, became inland places. Bruges did not try to reopen a seaway until our century, when a canal was dug to a point on the sea called Zeebrugge, or Bruges-on-the Sea. The project, which involved dredging a harbor and protecting it from silting, took eleven years to carry out; it was finished only a few years before World War I began. The German invaders used Zeebrugge to shelter their submarine fleet. One dark night, the British navy bottled in the submarines by sinking three old battleships across the harbor entrance and destroying installations with heavy bombardments.

A port was dredged out again after the war and the breakwater replaced, just in time to be finished for World War II. Zeebrugge was wrecked a second time, so thoroughly that repairs were not completed until 1951. Now for the third time in less than fifty years a canal connects Bruges with Zeebrugge, a port which many think will in time outrank both Antwerp and Ghent.

The new canal bypasses Damme, and the old waterway carries only pleasure or sightseeing boats. A road along the canal, shaded by poplars and willows, is so short and straight that the belfry of Bruges never disappears across the fields. Damme scarcely stirs; it has few inhabitants, and visitors come only occasionally to see the town hall, pretty as a toy, with high roof, gabled windows, and statues ornamenting the façade. Some tourists eat lunch or dinner in one of the taverns whose signs creak in the sea breeze.

The church looks much too big for the town. Its brick walls have already fallen in places. It has been grand; here Philip the Good married his Portuguese princess and, years later, their son Charles the Bold married Princess Margaret of York, who was to be the mother of Mary of Burgundy.

The great name in Damme belongs to someone who never lived there, who may never have lived at all. Tyl Ulenspiegl was a German and Netherlandish folklore hero long before the Flem-

The town hall of Damme.

ish writer Charles de Coster made him the main character in a
novel named in his honor and gave him Damme for a native
town. *The Legend of Tyl Ulenspiegl,* the long novel de Coster
wrote in French because he did not know Flemish correctly, is a
bit of Flamingant propaganda. Until de Coster adopted Tyl, the
fellow had been known chiefly for rough pranks and quick wits.
Writers down the years had invented adventures for him, but he
was always a rascal. De Coster reformed him or at least gave him
some noble traits, making him into a loyal Netherlander and set-
ting him down in the sixteenth century to suffer and struggle
against the tyranny of Philip II of Spain. De Coster turned the
scamp into a national hero, yet under the fine, patriotic coat Tyl
keeps the heart of a rogue.

The story is bitter, coarse, and cluttered with tiresome discus-
sions and preaching. It limps along under the author's burden of
philosophy and sometimes lies down and dies. Yet the author fascinates with this tale of men and women of Damme, of Bruges, of
Sluis, who drink too much, gorge on food, betray one another in a
world of superstition and belief in witchcraft. It is not Tyl and
his friends and enemies who give the book its strange charm, but
rather the land of Flanders. No one could write of his country
with more understanding than de Coster; he catches the mood of
every season: "April when fruit trees bloom"; "May with a clear
blue sky"; "September when the gnats stop biting." The reader
feels the warm spring wind, chills in a white world of snow falling
on ships off the Flemish coast. De Coster makes Flanders real and
beloved; he helps one understand Flemish pride in the land.

12

In Wallonia

Train service from Brussels to Wallonia is less than half as frequent as to Flanders, so it is easier to travel there by car, making overnight trips. Tournai lies fifty miles southwest of Brussels and is even nearer the French city of Lille, which in the Middle Ages was also a Belgian town. Roads are good, running between orchards and fields and past farmhouses, each surrounded like a rural fortress by out-buildings about a courtyard. Sometimes the farmsteads are painted yellow, green, or pink, a relief from the eternal red brick of Flanders.

A two-hour drive brings one to sight of the five towers of the cathedral that announces Tournai from across the plain. The church, one of the finest, oldest—and coldest—in Europe, is architecturally interesting, yet sightseers who think it striking from afar find the interior disappointing. Massive proportions destroy the illusion of size and space which delicate arches and slender pillars would give to a building of the same size. Nothing inside the cathedral is truly beautiful except the brilliant stained-glass windows.

The Grand'Place, where the cathedral stands, was almost destroyed in 1940, but the square has been carefully restored. Behind the cathedral and quite separate from it rises the oldest bell

The cathedral of Tournai, with its five bell towers.

tower in Belgium. Like the cathedral, it escaped air attacks that wrecked twelve thousand houses. New houses in the old style replace those that were destroyed; their bright red brick has begun to soften in color.

Tournai seems a quiet place of wide, clean streets, parks, and gardens. It keeps busy and is rich, too, with carpet works which export even to the United States, and craftsmen who carve the dark blue stone quarried nearby into statues and baptismal fonts for churches.

Tournai has a long, proud, and complicated history. One of the two most ancient cities in Belgium—Tongeren in the province of Limburg, pointing to burial mounds of Roman soldiers, claims to be older—Tournai also flourished in Roman days on the road from Cologne in Germany to the sea. Early kings of France, born in Tournai, governed lands to the south and east from this, their capital. Several are buried here. The tomb of one ruler, when opened in the seventeenth century yielded three hundred gold bees which had adorned his mantel. The idea of the golden bee so appealed to Napoleon Bonaparte that when he made himself emperor, he adopted the golden bee as his emblem.

During the Middle Ages, Tournai often belonged to France. It is the only city in Belgium to have been an English possession; King Henry VIII of England held it six years while he called himself King of France and England. Before Henry's time, Tournaisians supported Joan of Arc in her fight to make the timid dauphin king of France. In gratitude for their help she invited them to send three representatives to the city of Rheims when the dauphin was crowned king. The story goes that upon the return of these men, their fellow townsmen crowded before the cathedral to hear a report on the ceremony, to ask how Joan looked and what she said and did. When the English took her prisoner, Tournai sent her a purse containing gold pieces as a sign of affection.

The cathedral, the belfry, the tower of King Henry VIII, and the Pont des Trous, a bridge, tell of the past. The church and the tower have a sturdy air, but belfry and bridge look worn out. The tower near the river might be the donjon of an English fortress incorporated into fortifications around the city; it alone recalls Henry's stay in Tournai. It gives an impression of strength even now, with walls said to be twenty-one feet thick. Grass grows high on earth covering the rounded roof. By comparison, the much older Pont des Trous spanning the River Escaut seems frail. From the thirteenth century on, this arched bridge, ending in a tower on each bank, has formed part of Tournai's defense.

Having just left France, the river keeps its French name of Escaut until it enters Flanders, only a few miles to the northwest. There it becomes the Schelde, or Scheldt, and grows heavy with traffic. Here it is lazy. An occasional barge slips under the Pont des Trous. Three or four others are usually tied up at the cobbled wharf below. Lines of washing drape *Mon Rêve* (My Dream) from Mons; a woman polishes windows in the pilot house of *Kamina* from Ghent; a man fishes from the stern of the *Gazenia* out of Rotterdam.

One road from Tournai, through Ath, home of the giants, passes near Beloeil, the estate of the Prince de Ligne. The castle, more beautiful than the royal palace at Laeken, is the finest property in Belgium. Some compare its three hundred acres of gardens to those of Versailles. The grounds, laid out in formal French style, have smooth lawns, paths under arching branches, avenues of purple beech trees, walks between hedges clipped higher than a man's head, a lake that reflects the lime and chestnut trees shading its banks. A wide moat hems in the castle at the head of the lake; water laps at the rose brick foundations and big carp dart up into the sunlight.

Since the prince and his family open all of the castle except their private apartments, visitors may, for a small fee, wander through the gardens as well as rooms full of fine furniture, tapestries, paintings, and books and manuscripts, all gathered by generations of the de Lignes, a family well known in Belgian and European history.

Tournai is much farther from Liège than from Brussels or from Lille in France. Nevertheless, southeastern Wallonia, including

Liège, also deserves a visit. Liège, the city, has been called the Pittsburgh of Belgium and the Ardent City. These names apply because at night the sky reddens from the glow of blast furnaces and foundries. It long ranked as the industrial center of the nation. Sportsmen pay large prices for firearms made there. The first locomotive manufactured on the European continent came from works established by William Cockerill, the son of an English engineer, who set up spinning and weaving mills there. Until recently, miners dug coal around and inside the town. Most veins are exhausted by now, yet ugly slag heaps raise a reminder of the dead or dying industry. Occasionally a neighborhood in the city suffers a cave-in due to some empty mine pit below.

Although Liège has no Grand'Place, it gives space to wooded parks. The houses look sooty; few are beautiful, but many have splendid interiors. Museums and churches contain collections of valuable paintings. Liège also takes pride in its museums of archeology, decorative arts, and folk art of the region. A few buildings recall the gallant and tempestuous local history. City and province have not always formed part of Belgium. The finest structure, once the palace of the prince-bishop, now houses the law courts. Dark waters of the Meuse curve through town carrying tugboats, barges, and some pleasure boats. Though so near the German border, Liège is the most completely French city in Belgium. The scientific schools of its French-language university excel.

The road from Liège south into the Ardennes winds past streams that gush in narrow valleys or thread down hillsides, between stands of oak and spruce, where a castle turret or a church spire pierces the woodlands. Almost at the French frontier it reaches Bouillon, a valley town that looks much larger than a place of ten thousand inhabitants, because many imposing villas rise on the hillsides. The Semois River, so wild before it flows through Bouillon, twists quietly here between avenues of lime trees. On one side cultivated fields slope upward; on another, at the top of a cliff bulks the Castle of Bouillon, once the home fortress of the lords of Bouillon. Godfrey, the fifth ruler of his family, is a Belgian hero who actually lived, although he has crept into folklore, too. His grandfather is said to have been that Swan Knight, Lohengrin, who disembarked from an enchanted boat at Antwerp. Godfrey sold the castle and its domains to the prince-bishop of Liège in order to raise money to equip the army of forty thousand knights and foot soldiers he led on the First Crusade in 1096. When the Crusaders captured Jerusalem from the Saracens, they chose Godfrey their king of Jerusalem. He accepted the duty but was too pious to assume a royal title, saying he could not be king in a city where Christ had suffered humiliation and death.

The prince-bishop soon lost Bouillon to an ambitious, warlike family that, in turn, saw it taken by France. Indeed, the duchy, as it had come to be called, returned to the Netherlands only after the Battle of Waterloo.

The castle exemplifies the finest in medieval fortress building. Its defense begins with drawbridges over a moat, now dry, Low, vaulted stone passages lead to store rooms, guard rooms, dungeons, torture chambers, and an arsenal. During their rule of the United Netherlands, the Dutch used the arsenal and storerooms; rulers before them had often strengthened the fortress. A bell hanging in a belfry rang out alarms; a high observation post hollowed from the stone walls and said to date from Godfrey's time overlooks both the road from Liège and that from France. A well inside the fort supplied water enough for the defenders to endure any siege.

North from Bouillon stretches the valley of the Meuse, the heartland of Wallonia. Here the river absorbs numerous tributar-

The castle of Bouillon is over one thousand years old.

ies. Dinant, with its main street along one bank of the Meuse, has a church—often seen in photographs of Belgium—topped by an onion-shaped slate dome and wedged behind tall houses along the river. High white limestone cliffs crowd church and houses. Dinant craftsmen learned to beat out fine copper—and silver too—in Roman times. During the Middle Ages, its dinanderies (decorative or household utensils) were exported to England, France, Italy, Spain.

Namur, still farther north on the road to Brussels, is an eighteenth-century city, because invasions and battles destroyed all traces of its medieval past. However, it is charming, occupying a site that rises to the citadel hill which overlooks the juncture of the Meuse with a narrow tributary, the Sambre. Namur seems a pleasant town of cream-colored houses with wrought-iron balconies, shops that sell copper pans and bowls and a regional food specialty, the *couque,* a gingerbread cake. Citizens insist that their casino is one of the gayest in Europe. The people of Namur do not want heavy industry to darken skies and smudge building walls; they are content to live in a provincial town called the gateway to the Ardennes.

In the streets, townsfolk speak a Walloon dialect. A taxi driver may not know French well enough to serve as a guide to town landmarks. Belgians claim that the Walloon of Namur differs from that of Liège, while Tournai uses a third dialect. At the same time, a Walloon is indignant at the suggestion that his tongue is a fractured speech like Flemish.

Rain-washed summer air in the Ardennes is delicious, but winter brings bitter cold. Tourists, who supply the greatest income to the region, vanish. Inhabitants, shut in by snow-clogged roads and days of sleet, hibernate in their villages, with time to recall old tales of werewolves, of packs of infernal hunting dogs baying on dark nights, of castles and groves haunted by the devil. The younger people deny that such superstitions exist, and certainly radio has helped to frighten off ghosts and devils. Nevertheless, the Ardennes will be long in forgetting one cycle of legends; for centuries the region has taken pride in being the home of the Four Sons of Aymon and their magic horse Bayard.

The four brothers, Renaud, Richard, Alard, and Guichard, have starred in national folklore for a thousand years. They sit all four together on their enormous horse in every parade of giants through a Belgian city, whether in Flanders or Wallonia. Nevertheless, being natives of the Ardennes, they haunt the banks of the Meuse. The river road near Dinant passes through a rock split from the cliff which is called Bayard's Rock because Bayard is supposed to have shattered the cliff with a single blow of his hoof while carrying his riders to safety.

According to legend, the brothers were nobles at the court of the Emperor Charlemagne, who had knighted all of them in a single ceremony. They swore to be his loyal vassals but broke their oath and rebelled, like true Belgians, against what they believed to be injustice. With the help of a cousin who could work magic, they made the emperor come to terms with them, an exploit that endears them to Belgium. Not so long ago one could find in shops in little towns a book printed in big type on coarse paper, which told their story in simple words. Such a work had been popular for generations. It might be impossible to discover one anywhere now, yet from time to time modern authors rework the plot of the tale. In 1941, during World War II when the Germans were occupying Belgium, a popular Belgian playwright, Herman Closson, used the theme as inspiration for *The Play of the Sons of Aymon*. A troupe of young actors, who had begun their association as a group of Boy Scouts, performed the work in small Walloon towns and big cities. In the last scene two singers chant, "Fiery land of blood, they are alive, your sons of Aymon." This drama of struggle, these words of defiance roused so many public demonstrations by the audiences against the invaders that Nazi authorities banned the play. Closson merely changed the title to *Horse Bayard,* and his actors went right on playing it around the country.

13

La Capitale

Visitors who knew Brussels ten or twenty years ago find it much changed and realize it keeps on growing very fast and changing.

The Grand'Place remains one of the finest town squares in Europe, yet it has been invaded by traffic and sightseers. Its city hall, topped by a tower as delicate as spun sugar on a wedding cake, takes up almost all of one side of the square. By day all the buildings look like a dream fantasy; by night, when illuminated, the square becomes even more fascinating, for tall houses of the guild of brewers, painters, boatmen line the place. They show gilded façades; their dark Spanish-tiled roofs lift into a welter of television antennae. Stone and gilt metal figures—stars, birds, animals, and ships—decorate each step-gabled roof.

No private cars may park on the square but tourist buses crowd half of it, while traffic races through at high speed. One risks his life crossing from the sidewalk to the flower and bird markets which once seemed such leisurely places. Masses of sightseers mill about the stalls that sell anemones, tulips, roses, or chrysanthemums. They jam the area where wooden bird cages are stacked one upon the other. The overall view is a kaleidoscope of green, purple, yellow, and orange.

The bird market is held only on Sunday. Here one buys canaries or snowy Japanese sparrows with jet-black eyes and black beaks, or wee brown Bengalis with bright red beaks. In larger cages white cockatoos preen their feathers. One sees lovebirds and varieties of pigeons: fantail, pouter, and especially racing pigeons.

Pigeon racing remains one of Belgium's favorite sports, vying in popularity with soccer and with bicycle, motorcycle, and car racing. The nation is said to have more pigeons than the rest of Europe all together. Some birds cost thousands of francs; thousands more go out in bets on weekly races. On Saturdays, the radio announces where and when the birds will be released from the large willow baskets in which "conveyors" have carried them to a starting point, perhaps as far away as North Africa. On Sunday, weather reports come every hour describing weather along the route the birds will take on their flight to home lofts. The winner, of course, covers the greatest distance in the best time.

The Grand'Place recalls the dukes of Burgundy and their tournaments here, but it also speaks of archers, carpenters, butchers, and men of other corporations who sat in the houses they built around the square. Guilds were the strength of Netherlands cities. Certainly much the same spirit survives in our days of big business firms and glass-and-steel office buildings. To be convinced of this close association, one has only to watch the *boursiers* in a hotel not far from the Grand'Place. Such groups of business and professional men are said to be important not only in Brussels but also in cities like Antwerp and Liège.

In Brussels they meet every Wednesday at a big hotel for a conference, then lunch together according to occupation. Engineers sit at one long table, brewers at another; here are glass manufacturers, there oil men. Two or three wholesale junk dealers have a small table to themselves. Many drift into the dining room after the others have begun lunch; they shake hands with their colleagues, sit down, and order what they want. Soon tables are cluttered with food of all kinds and at all stages of a meal: chops near cheese, fried shrimp beside apricot tarts, heaps and heaps of *Frites* (fried potatoes), bowls of fruit, glasses of beer side by side with pitchers of wine or bottles of mineral water, in an array of objects like a Flemish still life. The men around the tables, their faces flushed and animated, could sit for Brueghel or Rubens. One imagines them in the velvet and fur-edged cloaks of their ancestors, feasting against a background of gilt-leather walls in a guild house. By the way, in Brussels even the ruddiest, most Flemish-looking men usually speak French. One authority states that four-fifths of the Bruxellois speak French as their first language, whatever their ethnic heritage.

If the tourist explores the Grand'Place on a fine day, he may want to sit at one of the sidewalk cafes which, along with restau-

A sidewalk cafe
on the Grand'Place.

rants, curio stores, and lace shops, occupy the ground floor of most guild houses. It will be a noisy scene to be sure. Looking beyond traffic and up to the statue of Saint Michael atop the town hall, one may see a wedding party go into or emerge from the building. In its Marriage Room, the visitor may watch a civil wedding, the service which must precede every church wedding in Belgium. On Saturdays the ceremony is performed free, and bridal couples line up. They sit with friends on long benches waiting for their turn. Ushers solemnly escort bride and groom to the platform where a city official, representing the mayor, marries them. Each ceremony lasts about ten minutes; at the end, the newlyweds and their witnesses sign the register and, as a new pair takes their place, leave by red-carpeted steps leading to the Lion's Staircase, a short flight of steps guarded at street level by two stone lions.

Mannekin Pis, the oldest inhabitant of Brussels, has an address nearby. Foreigners and Belgian tourists alike go to see him standing above his fountain. The *Mannekin Pis* is a small bronze figure of a baby boy whose uninhibited attitude enchants visitors. All Belgium shares an amused interest in the little fellow, and he so delighted foreigners in the past that they kidnapped him. English soldiers carried him away in the eighteenth century. Scarcely had he returned before French troops made off with him. This time the king of France sent him home with the title of *chevalier,* or knight, along with a white satin suit embroidered in gold. This outfit, yellowed by time, hangs with most of his wardrobe in glass cases of a room in the city museum across the Grand'Place from the town hall. Models display his other suits. For a Belgian festival he may appear as a bullfighter, a Sioux Indian, an Inca from Peru, a Gille of Binche, or a Scotch laddie in kilts.

Brussels, the old town built on low ground, still keeps here and there a Flemish atmosphere. In the Marolles, a working-class sub-

Mannekin Pis, Brussels.

urb at the foot of the hill below the higher part of the city, one occasionally hears in the narrow, crowded streets a distinctive patois which mixes French and Flemish, together. This speech is disappearing now as standard Flemish and French are diffused by schools and the radio. The Marolles's other claim to notice is that Peter Brueghel lived, died, and is buried here. Here stands his well-restored brick gabled house. Although always a city man, he must have often gone into the surrounding countryside of Brabant to paint farm laborers, peasant revels, and village scenes.

Not so long ago a short walk from a large downtown hotel led to picturesque shops, like the *droguerie* on the corner of the Street of the Swallows, which sold American detergents, rope, and fly poison, but not drugs. One bought aspirin and had doctors' prescriptions filled in a *pharmacie* on the Street of the Flowers. A ruined tower presided over the neighborhood of small shops and gabled houses with smoking chimney pots. Now the tower is all that remains of this ancient clutter. It has been saved because once it formed part of the city's defenses. Now it is jammed between ugly new buildings and dwarfed by large very modern ones. Perhaps it will be jolted by vibrations from trains soon to run in subway tunnels dug out nearby.

The ground beneath Brussels is slimy and treacherous for, in the beginning, this was a water city like Ghent and Brugge. The Grand'Place is reputed to occupy the site of an ancient marsh. A little river, the Senne, once crawled through a dilapidated slum downtown. Now traffic careens or cars park in avenues and esplanades covering the vaulted-over river and the old canals. Firewood Quay and Quay of Building Stones are street names which tell of wharves used before canals were filled and the river caged. Anyone who wants to see what Brussels looked like a hundred or more years ago may examine a series of small paintings hanging in the town hall; they were made before the river was covered over and the slum torn down. However, since no self-respecting Belgian town feels complete without a port and water traffic, Brussels does have a canal on which barges carry oil, textiles, machinery, and manufactured goods back and forth between the industrial city of Charleroi to the south and Antwerp to the north.

A short car ride separates Brussels from a mechanical wonder of this century. A few miles beyond Waterloo, near the village of Ronquières, a sightseeing boat offers the strangest ride imaginable. The boat follows barges through the muddy water of a canal that cuts the flat landscape until suddenly, ahead, two slim towers spring from mid-canal, each sending green, many-windowed wings across the water. Several barges along with the boat, approach a container which looks like a giant coal gondola on a railroad. This container opens and swallows boat and barges into its watery hold and, as they float there, very slowly lifts them up the Inclined Plain (or Ship Incline) of Ronquières, a distance of nearly a mile, to a man-made lock where water flows through a concrete bed or channel carried high above ground—a car can be driven underneath the artificial canal bed supported by three hundred-foot-high pillars. Reaching the higher canal, the red container opens to disgorge boat and barges. The barges slip out for their journey on to Charleroi, while the sightseeing boat joins barges bound for Brussels, to be lowered by the same mechanism to plain level. The towers contain electronic devices which work the gondolas, and spectators may watch the whole operation from windows of the green arms across the water. This amazing piece of engineering, like nothing else in the world, does credit to Belgian and Swedish engineers who designed and built it. It shortens the canal route by many miles. Since its opening in 1968 it has not paid for itself, yet Belgium feels such an important aid to heavy water traffic plying through the country will in time be profitable.

In medieval times, strong walls guarded the lower city of Brussels, just as elsewhere in the Netherlands. A few fragments of wall and two towers of these fortifications stand isolated in the present. When the Cathedral of Saint Michael was begun on the slope leading from old Brussels to the hill above, it stood outside the walls. That was eight hundred years ago, in Burgundian times. But three centuries went by before the church was completed and the entire structure underwent restoration in the nineteenth century. Guidebooks and maps name it the Cathedral of Saint Michael, but the Bruxellois call it Sainte Gudule for a favorite woman saint whose relics are said to be there. Generations of Netherlands rulers have been baptized, married, and buried in the church. Here Belgians celebrated victory and sought consolation in defeat. More than once under German occupation the congregation rose and sang with the organ as it pealed out the music of the forbidden national anthem, "La Brabançonne."

The windows constitute a portrait gallery of Netherlands royalty from the sixteenth century on. Jewellike glass shows Mary of Burgundy and Maximilian of Austria, Charles V and Philip II of Spain, as well as Albert and Isabella. The archduchess and her husband are buried in the chapel lighted by a window picturing them together.

The Square du Sablon (Square of the Little Sandhill) is not far from the cathedral. This most unforgettable open space in a city of many beautiful parks tilts green lawns and flower beds uphill towards the statues of the Counts of Egmont and Hoorne. Refusing to join their friend Prince William of Orange when he revolted against Philip II, these men remained loyal to Spain and the established Roman Catholic religion. Yet they dared to protest the Inquisition and the cruelties of Philip's governor, the Duke of Alva. For this, the latter took revenge by having them beheaded on the Grand'Place before the town hall.

Statues of Belgian scholars and scientists line each side of the park, but the most unusual guardians are forty-eight small men in bronze who rise at intervals from the railing that encloses the square. These figures represent the forty-eight guilds of old Brussels. The baker carries loaves under his arm and a shovel for raking bread from the oven, the miller stands beside a miniature windmill, the artist holds a palette, the fisherman dangles a string of fish.

The church just above the square uphill, Our Lady of Victories, was a gift of the crossbowmen, another reminder of the importance of these "unions" in Belgian history. Almost every church in the city possesses at least one painting, statue, or stained-glass window given by a guild.

At the foot of Our Lady of Victories, an antiques fair goes on all day Saturday and on Sunday mornings. In fine weather, or even in a drizzle, crowds press into the aisles between booths:

Belgians, of course, of all types; Japanese tourists, English, French, and Americans examine and buy. Untidy youths elbow distinguished men who look to be true collectors. On a fine May morning, women in long fur coats stand beside other women in blue jeans. Music blares from a rock group seated on a platform. One dealer presides over his wares dressed in a white satin suit— knee breeches, embroidered coat—and white wig. Old copper, pewter, porcelain, family portraits, prints and etchings, a mahogany chest, or horoscopes in verse, all are here to be bought—at a price. The Flea Market on a nearby square offers what looks like junk: one sees broken chairs and heaped-up faded rugs, old garments and battered cooking pans. However, the true collector will go early to Ball Game Square, where the selling takes place, and he will dig out treasures that cost only a few francs—perhaps a piece of fine Val St. Lambert glass or a square of good tapestry, probably the unworn part of a threadbare wall hanging.

Upper Brussels on the hill is a handsome city in itself. The royal palace, which appears somber and heavy from the front, overlooks a stretch of wooded garden in the rear. The Houses of Parliament stand here, as well as the Royal Library and the Royal Conservatory of Music. Three years out of every four, the latter building is the site of the Queen Elizabeth Music Competition, one of the most important musical contests anywhere. Initiated by Queen Elizabeth, wife of Albert I of Belgium, in 1937, it was known at first as the Ysaye Musical Contest, honoring the Belgian violinist, Eugene Ysaye. That first year, the winner of the competition was the Russian violinist David Oistrakh. In 1950, the queen changed the name of the affair to the Queen Elizabeth Music Competition. In May of the first year of a four-year cycle, violinists are judged three times; judges eliminate some of the entrants each time until the final winner plays against eleven others. The same procedure is followed the following May, with pianists trying to win. The third year, young composers play music they have written. The fourth year, for some reason, no contest is held. Every musician covets first prize, for it means not only a sum of money but engagements for concerts and often international fame. From the initiation of the contests, that is from 1937, until 1968, three Americans had won first prize. Russia counts the largest number of top winners, including, besides Oistrakh, the well-known pianist Emil Gilels.

A sightseer who is not distracted by cars dashing out, making sudden turns and unexpected stops, may admire the well-paved boulevards that fan out in many directions. Some of these "freeways" are divided down the center by tree-shaded esplanades wide enough to accommodate parked cars as well as streetcar tracks down which some elderly trolley rattles. Often, to left or right rises a grassy slope of park. In spring and summer the grounds are shaded, ducks or swans float on ponds, and flower borders color the scene. Fruit trees flower madly in April and May; chestnut trees bloom in May; pines mingle with walnut and beech trees. The Forest of Soignes, not far from Waterloo, borders the road with miles of tall, splendid copper beeches.

The Avenue of Tervuren leads to the Royal Museum for Central Africa. This drive is a must, not only because a forest shades the way, but also because, among all the rich museums in Brussels, this one is unique. King Leopold II, who founded it, left to his chilly, rainy country—it rains about two days out of every three in Belgium—an enchanted spot, a hot and exotic bit of a different world. The large rooms of the museum display carved wood and ivory, cloth woven in brilliant patterns, African canoes, fans, daggers, grotesque masks, beaded headdresses. Glass cases show larger-than-life plants of the Congo, like cinnamon, cotton, and many flowers and fruits. Also on display are Henry Stanley's worn canteen, his spyglasses, long-handled pistol, his sextant and compass. A bronze plaque showing the profile of Leopold II in low relief bears these lines (in French) written by the Belgian historian Henri Pirenne: "From the high windows of his palace at Ostend, he, like Henry the Navigator, let his imagination roam far over the water."

14

This and That About Belgium

Flemings and Walloons alike feel that Brussels belongs to them. The brickmaker from the polder country, the carpet or tapestry worker from Tournai, the soldier stationed on the citadel above Namur, a professor from the University of Liège, all think nothing of driving or taking a train into the capital for a banquet, a parade, a visit with friends. Sports fans flock from kilometers around to see the national soccer team play in a city stadium —half these spectators carry a raincoat or umbrella, just in case the day turns into one of the two rainy days out of three. Residents of Leuven, Mechelen, Ghent, and Antwerp commute to work in Brussels; in Bruges, many park cars or bicycles near the railroad station and take the sixty-minute train ride to schools and jobs in the capital.

Inasmuch as Brussels is truly the heart of Belgium, it is understandable that city shops offer every regional product from wooden shoes and Ostend sole to Val Saint Lambert glass, Dinant copperware and the small, hard black balloon candies made in Tournai, which Tournaisians claim will cure a cold. The capital serves dishes from French cookbooks as well as Flemish specialties and food characteristic of the Ardennes.

When the first supermarket opened in Brussels not too long

ago, two American women living in the capital were so delighted that they went first thing on opening morning to shop. They bought madly; when they wheeled their filled carts to the checker's counter a group of television cameramen met them and asked them to put aside their own carts and go through the motions of filling empty ones. This they did, the photographers following them as they went and catching them when they checked through with the make-believe purchases. Films of their activities made Belgian television that evening. Since then, supermarkets have appeared in many Brussels neighborhoods as well as in other cities. The capital and one or two other towns have some modern malls which entice shoppers to stores, tearooms, displays of old cars, or modern statues. After all, the idea of a covered shopping area is not new; of course a mall is heated and, if necessary cooled, but the mall is really a present-day improvement over the long, covered arcades or passages so numerous in Brussels, where small shops have long sold many kinds of merchandise.

A Belgian supermarket holds the interest of a day-to-day museum because of the variety of foods displayed: dozens of different kinds of sausage; pickled or jellied eels; cheese from France, Switzerland, Holland, and Germany as well as excellent Belgian cheese. One finds Ardennes ham; Mechelen asparagus and great sweet strawberries (in season); pale pink carrots no longer than a finger; cauliflower, which costs about one-fifth as much as in the United States; and Belgian chicory or endive, so hard to find in American stores. Belgians like to eat heartily and well so they are willing to pay for good meals. A workingman's family spends a large part of his wages on food, yet Belgian wages are excellent by European standards.

Some recipes may seem new to American cooks, like Flemish *cramique,* a sweet bread, yellow with eggs and full of raisins. The *couques* of Dinant and Namur are gingerbread cut out and

Traditionally, shrimp fishing has been done on horseback.

stamped on top with designs of ferns, grapes, apples, dogs. The people in Sint-Truiden like a thick cinnamon-flavored cherry soup. Flemish pancakes are stiff with a glaze of caramelized sugar. Other delicacies include carp baked in white wine, with mushrooms and onions added; wild boar served with chestnuts; ham tarts, cheese tarts, waffles. Ghent invented the *waterzooi,* chicken stewed with herbs, white wine, and butter; fish waterzooie consists of a mixture of eel, carp, and bream (a kind of whitefish), cut up and boiled with butter, herbs, and onions. And above all, everywhere, Belgians eat *frites,* their long, thin, usually crisp version of what we call French-fried potatoes.

As to beer, the country drinks more per person than Germany. For centuries each locality has brewed its special brand: blond beer or black or golden; or *krick,* a ruby-red type flavored with cherries, bottled like wine, and left to settle for two years. There are sweetish beers, beers made from hops, and *geuze,* which ferments from a combination of hops and grapes and which besides being a delicious beverage is preferred by housewives for cooking. Grape growers in Brabant make their own white wine but if one tries to order a bottle in a restaurant, the waiter explains, "We have none of that stuff." Belgians drink French, German, Spanish wines.

This nation of beer drinkers also eats tons of delicious chocolate candy. The capital and all large cities have countless *confiseries* (candy shops), while smaller towns almost always have one or two. Lingering before a counter in a confiserie it is hard to choose from the array of *pralines,* or chocolates (not the brown sugar nut candies we call by that name). Chocolate baskets, hearts, leaves, bells, mushrooms, flowers, and tinsel-wrapped mysteries all look tempting as they wait to be arranged in a gold-paper box, tied with gold or silver cord, and delivered to the buyer like treasure —candies are very expensive in Belgium.

In the country, even occasionally in the suburbs of Brussels, Ghent, or Liège, men wear wooden shoes. They probably work a vegetable garden or among plants in a nursery. Farmers in their muddy fields need wooden shoes and so do lace makers, who put them on over heavy woolen socks to protect their feet from icy stone or brick floors as they sit, hour after hour, at their tedious craft. When newly varnished a bright yellow, the shoes look strong enough to last months of wear, but they are fashioned from such soft wood that they quickly scrape through; farmers may have to buy new ones as often as once a month.

A few years ago the bicycle was the Belgian workhorse on roads and streets; now it is giving way to the automobile. The nation manufactures no brand of its own, but a thousand German Fords a day roll off the assembly line at Genk in Limburg. And in Antwerp two General Motors plants put together about half a million cars and trucks a year—all foreign makes for which they have sales rights. The Swedish Volvo and the French Renault, among other European motors, also come from Belgian assembly lines.

Few American automobiles mingle in the swarms of small cars that infest streets and roads, for they use too much gasoline which remains expensive compared to United States prices, even with oil refineries in Ghent and Antwerp. Only since 1969 has a motorist been obliged to pass a driver's license test. Some pre-1969 drivers indulge in strange practices, including high speed; many seem urged on by a compulsion to get everywhere first.

Belgians work hard at their jobs and in their homes and pretty gardens, yet they find time and energy to read and to enjoy life in other ways. They know more about us than we about them, probably because, as a small nation, they follow events abroad which may affect their own fate. Moreover, the role their government plays in the many international organizations with headquarters among them stimulates their interest and concern.

As to enjoyment, they have zest for it. The nation observes eleven legal holidays every year; the United States has five. They celebrate a saint's day, a historical or folklore anniversary from village to metropolis, taking the trouble to hang out flags and banners, parading, attending High Mass, crowding into carnivals, and watching pageants. One seaside resort mounts a parade of giant shrimp. A large Flemish city sees an annual procession of enormous cats go down its streets. In the Ardennes town of Saint Hubert, named for the patron saint of hunters, the citizens wear red coats and listen to hunting horns sound all during his feast day. The Gilles of Binche have made their festival hilarious and famous. The world knows about the procession and pageant of the Holy Blood in Bruges, about the wedding of the giants of Ath, the march of the penitents in the Spanish spirit of Veurne. Every July, the Ommegang on the Brussels Grand'Place recalls the fourteenth-century gift of a miracle-working statue of the Blessed Virgin to our Our Lady of Victories near the Sablon Square. Several thousand men, women, and young people turn the Ommegang into a spectacle of sixteenth-century magnificence: silks, velvets, coronets, armor and fine swords, bright banners, and pike-bearing soldiers of that period. Now, Belgians observe Mother's Day and Father's Day as carefully as people in the United States.

Although they so love their own country that they rarely emigrate to other lands, they quickly adopt foreign ideas which they believe to be useful. They also give ideas to foreigners. Psychiatrists and doctors concerned with mental illness know about the Flemish town of Geel, where they find the approach to such problems humane and generally successful. The rather severe-looking small town has long received disturbed or mentally retarded persons into the homes of local families. Once the sufferer has been medically certified as harmless, he becomes a paying guest in a home where he leads a normal life. If able, he goes out to work on a farm or in the town at some job he is capable of doing. One notices odd-looking people on the streets of Geel—a vacant-faced young man washing a car in front of a commercial garage; an elderly woman who talks to herself us she totters down the street with a net shopping bag hanging over her arm. The Geel project is no longer an experiment. It has proved that kindness and as near a normal life as possible benefit the emotionally disturbed more than any institution can.

The fashion now is for critics to maintain that Belgium's very receptiveness to foreign influence shows that no true national culture prevails, only a Flemish spirit and a French outlook on life. These skeptics insist that no literature can be called Belgian. At first glance, such claims seem true. Writers in Netherlandish publish excellent novels, yet a work written in Dutch finds fewer readers and is less often translated into other languages than a novel in French, because Dutch is less widely used than French or English. We who speak English rarely know Flemish and so hear little about Dutch-Flemish literature; few translations of such works appear. Flemish writers, or rather writers in Flemish, must compete with those of Holland for literary recognition, although in fact most famous "Belgian authors" have been Flemings who wrote in French: Maeterlinck, the poet Verhaeren and others. One sees good drama in Netherlandish performed in theaters of the Netherlands, in Brussels and in theaters of large cities of Flanders, but rarely elsewhere. On the other hand, Walloon writers and some Flemings who write in French may be confused with French authors; their plays always used to open in Paris. Lately, government-sponsored training for actors has produced excellent players who remain on the Belgian stage. Now Parisian critics frequently come to Brussels for the first night of a play being tried out there, if not by a Walloon or a French-writing Fleming, then the French translation of an English, German, or North American work.

Both Walloons and Flemings write well, with imagination and depth. We know only a few aside from Maeterlinck and Verhaeren. Henri Pirenne is a historian whose work on Belgium ranks as a classic and whose study of a medieval town seems the proper subject for a citizen of the land of brave towns. Georges Simenon, who was born in Liège but has long lived abroad in France, the United States, and Switzerland, interests hordes of readers throughout the world with his mystery stories and probing psychological novels. Françoise Mallet-Joris, a Flemish author who writes in French, now comes across to us in translations; she receives serious attention whenever her novels appear. Finally, Michel de Ghelderode, who, as he says, is "rooted" in the Flemish nation, also uses French for his strange works which concern themselves with human suffering and with death. Theaters in Belgium, in France, and indeed in many countries, including the United States, produce his plays. Thoughts of death obsess de Ghelderode, whereas Françoise Mallet-Joris, in her best-known work, *Lettre à Moi-Même* (Letter to Myself), after self-examination and analysis, concludes, "I love life." Both attitudes are typically Belgian.

After all, the claim that Belgium has no national culture or unity does not hold true. The following lines from a study of the nation's spirit express a view that seems far more perceptive than that of the pessimists. In a handbook, *The Contemporary Theatre*, published by the Belgian Institute of Information and Documentation, Luc Andre, a literary critic of renown, comes to this judgment:

> Belgium, despite the many efforts that have been made to divide it, survives as a nation, as a community sharing similar customs, ideas and ambitions. Willy nilly, the four to five million French-speaking Belgians live alongside their Flemish countrymen, and vice versa. Flemings, Walloons and Bruxellois (for there are three partners in this marriage) share the same viruses, the same customs and the same cultural reflexes.
>
> It is a fact that every Flemish writer has assimilated something of the French culture; that every Belgian author writing in French—even pure Walloons like Georges Simenon—have [sic] assimilated something Flemish.

Today, bickering arises from many internal problems. The Belgian form of government may become even more loosely federated than it is presently with even greater local autonomy. Who knows? Walloons and Flemings, nevertheless, cling to life in their common homeland. This is a family affair, as though two fine, ambitious brothers squabble in the same house and yet intend to make the place wiser and more prosperous.

Index

About the Author

Dorothy Loder was born in San Antonio, Texas. She is a graduate of the University of Texas and studied further at Columbia University, Brown University, and the Sorbonne. Mrs. Loder has traveled extensively in Europe and visited Belgium most recently in 1972. She lives in San Antonio, where she pursues her interests in gardening and history and is active in club work. Mrs. Loder is the author of another book in this series, *The Land and People of Spain*.

3

Th
WAI